MILITARY
ARCHITECTURE
at
FORT CLARK

MILITARY ARCHITECTURE at FORT CLARK

A GUIDE TO THE TEXAS HISTORIC LANDMARK

WILLIAM F. HAENN

Foreword by Colonel (Ret.) Thomas Ty Smith

THE
History
PRESS

Published by The History Press
Charleston, SC
www.historypress.com

Front cover, top row: Quartermaster Storehouse/Commissary, built in 1892. *Second row*: New Cavalry Barracks, built in 1932, home to soldiers of America's Greatest Generation. *Third row*: Palisado Building Kitchen/Mess Room, erected in 1869–70 by Buffalo Soldiers of the 25th Infantry. *Bottom row*: Staff Officers' Quarters, completed in 1888, once the residence of General George S. Patton Jr. *Back cover*: The Fort Clark Historic District, looking north, in 1946. *All cover photos by the author or from the author's collection.*

First published 2023

Manufactured in the United States

ISBN 9781467155564

Library of Congress Control Number: 2023945820

Notice: The information in this book is true and complete to the best of our knowledge. It is offered without guarantee on the part of the author or The History Press. The author and The History Press disclaim all liability in connection with the use of this book.

To
Francis Henry French, 19th U.S. Infantry,
a soldier of the Indian Wars who left us his diary,
and
Maynard H. McKinnon, a.k.a. Sergeant Mac, Ambulance Co. No. 7,
a soldier of the Great War who left us his letters,
and
Ernest H. Collier, 9th U.S. Cavalry,
a Buffalo Soldier of World War II who told us his story.

All served at Fort Clark and experienced these buildings.

CONTENTS

CONTENTS

FOREWORD

Established by the 1ˢᵗ Infantry in 1852 as part of the Second Federal Line, Fort Clark, Texas, served the nation and the Texas frontier for nearly a century. A key post protecting the Rio Grande boundary, Fort Clark played a pivotal role in the antebellum and post–Civil War Texas frontier Indian Wars, the border troubles of the Mexican Revolution, and in preparing our army for both World War I and World War II. Serving at the fort was a host of distinguished officers, including James Longstreet, John Bell Hood, J.E.B. Stuart, John L. Bullis, Ranald S. Mackenzie, William R. Shafter, Jonathan M. Wainwright, George C. Marshall and George S. Patton Jr. The post was also home to the Seminole-Negro Indian Scouts and the Buffalo Soldiers of the Ninth and Tenth Cavalry and of the Twenty-Fourth and Twenty-Fifth Infantry. Fort Clark remains one of the best preserved of the Texas frontier posts, with dozens of historic buildings in the Fort Clark Historic District that speak to our past.

No one is more qualified to capture the complex history of Fort Clark than author and historian William F. "Bill" Haenn. In my years of research and writing books and articles on the military history of Texas and the Southwest, if I had any question or issue concerning Fort Clark, I would immediately contact Bill for an accurate, thoughtful answer. A diligent scholar, he has amassed an assembly of primary documents, maps and photographs worthy of any archive, generously sharing his collection with other researchers and historians. As a retired army officer, and a resident of historic quarters at Fort Clark for over three decades, Bill is uniquely positioned to provide his keen insight and depth of knowledge in *Military Architecture at Fort Clark: A Guide to the Texas Historic Landmark*. The work is drawn from a rich variety of sources, such as the National Archives, War Department reports, U.S. Army inspection reports, monthly post returns, the National Register of Historic Places and significant personal memoirs. It is a definitive study and a first-rate benchmark example for scholars and historians.

Colonel (Ret.) Thomas Ty Smith, USA
San Antonio, Texas

ACKNOWLEDGEMENTS

It seems only yesterday that I was working on my first Arcadia Publishing book about Fort Clark, yet it has been over twenty years since my baptism as an author. In that length of time, several things have grown significantly: my collection of Fort Clark images, my knowledge of Fort Clark history and the number of Fort Clark's historical markers. For me, pursuing Fort Clark history is a daunting, thankless yet very worthwhile and rewarding undertaking. The reader may never have heard of Fort Clark. Its history went dark the year I was born, in 1946, when the fort was handed over to civilian ownership. In fact, nothing much positive can be said of the U.S. Army's own treatment of Fort Clark's history until Senior Army Chaplain Cephas C. Bateman of the 14th Cavalry wrote the first published "history" of Fort Clark for the December 20, 1913 issue of the *Army and Navy Register*. He titled his article "A Landmark of the Old Frontier—Fort Clark, Texas" and stated he had been afforded the "pleasure to rescue from official oblivion some facts concerning this historic post." In 1920, Chaplain Bateman updated and retitled his history of Fort Clark, publishing a pamphlet called *Modernized Outpost of the Old Frontier*. There are really only three published works specifically focused on the history of Fort Clark: *The Lonely Sentinel* by Caleb Pirtle III and Michael F. Cusack; my Arcadia Publishing book *Fort Clark and Brackettville, Land of Heroes*; and Don Swanson's *Chronicles of Fort Clark Texas*. Sadly, *The Lonely Sentinel* is nothing more than a screenplay and not well documented or accurately researched facts. Much of its made-up history continues to contaminate the genuine narrative.

My acknowledgements here are, first and foremost, of people I never met but to whom I owe an unpayable debt of gratitude. All of them unknowingly provided me with inspiration, encouragement and reward because Fort Clark was part of their life experience and they were thoughtful enough to record that experience in writing or with a camera. Also remembered and acknowledged are those unknown soldiers, masons, carpenters and quarrymen whose physical labors built the enduring examples of classic U.S. Army architecture chronicled in these pages.

First is Texas patriot Samuel A. Maverick, who claimed as his headright survey Las Moras Spring and the league of land that would become Fort Clark. Next are the inspecting officers who left us their descriptions and maps of the post: Lieutenant Colonel William G. Freeman (1853), Colonel Joseph K.F. Mansfield (1856 and 1860), Colonel Joseph E. Johnston (1859), Colonel Edmund Schriver (1873) and Colonel James R. Pourie (1928). Then come the authors of the indispensable firsthand accounts of everyday army life at Fort Clark recorded in their diaries, letters and memoirs: Lieutenant Francis H. French; Lieutenant William Paulding; Lieutenant Hugh S. Johnson; Post Surgeon John Vance Lauderdale; Assistant Post Surgeon Edgar Mearns; army wives Lydia Spencer Lane, Frances Mullen Boyd and Maria Brace Kimball; and Sergeant Maynard H. McKinnon. Not to be forgotten are the photographers who captured those prized moments in time that never fail to fascinate: C.D. Curtis; Assistant Surgeon Charles M. Gandy; Carl Ekmark; Eugene O. Goldbeck; Paul Hill; Herman Lippe; Walter M. Cline Jr.; Robert L. Warren; and the nameless U.S. Army Signal Corps photographers. Many of their memorable images of Fort Clark are included here to enhance the narrative and provide a window on another time.

Finally, a long-overdue thank-you to the Sisters of the Immaculate Heart of Mary and their open carry of heavy wooden rulers in the 1950s, which made me pay attention at the blackboard while learning to diagram a sentence or writing one hundred times, "I will not talk in class." I'm sure the good Sisters would be pleased with my acquired ability to construct a paragraph.

INTRODUCTION

Along the old stage road, now the border highway (U.S. 90), stretching west from San Antonio, there existed in the early days a line of forts or camps. As the settlers pushed out from the towns new posts were established only later to be abandoned, so that of all of these many posts dotted through Texas as shown on the older maps, remains only Fort Clark. —The Cavalry Journal, *1930*

Thomas Jefferson recognized that "a morsel of genuine history is a thing so rare as to be always valuable." Fort Clark, in Kinney County, Texas, is far more than a "morsel"—it is a full-course buffet of U.S. Army architecture, with scores of well-preserved structures from the nineteenth and twentieth centuries, some built to Quartermaster model plans and many of them the only surviving examples in the nation. While most other Texas antebellum and Indian War–era forts are long abandoned, reduced to nothing more than stark chimneys on the prairie or experienced extensive reconstruction and restoration, Fort Clark's wide-ranging military architecture has endured virtually unchanged. It continues to function as a modernized outpost of the old frontier. Fort Clark is an overlooked site, occupied by mankind for more than twelve thousand years and also indisputably entitled to over four centuries of recorded human endeavor; as a consequence, the site of Fort Clark quite possibly stands alone in the diverse multicultural and military heritage of America.

Fort Clark's prominent role in the shaping of Texas history spanned ninety-two years (1852–1944) while generations of its soldiers, officers and their families faithfully served the nation. This noteworthy service to the nation was accomplished entirely through the dedicated performance of duty by some of the U.S. Army's most distinguished leaders and units. Fort Clark's lineage of U.S. Army units serves as an honor roll of the army's most legendary cavalry and infantry regiments. More than thirty recipients of the Medal of Honor served at Fort Clark between 1852 and 1944, including four Seminole Scouts. All of the army's historic Black regiments served at Fort Clark, as well as the Seminole-Negro Indian Scouts and the 2nd Cavalry Division. No other post can claim a richer, more impressive or lengthier Buffalo Soldier legacy.

Today, more than 120 historic structures and sites built by the U.S. Army remain as testament and in tribute to that service to Texas and the nation. In December 1979, the Texas Historical Commission (THC) nominated the Fort Clark Historic District for inclusion in the National Register of Historic Places. Since being entered in the National Register, Fort Clark's rich military heritage and architecture have been recognized by the THC through the issuance of six Subject Markers (Fort Clark, 1994; Seminole Scout Camp on Fort Clark, 2002; 2nd Cavalry Division at Fort Clark, 2009; Original Post Cemetery, 2011; Las Moras Spring, 2013; and John Horse, 2014), fifteen Recorded Texas Historic Landmark Markers (Fort Clark Guardhouse, 1962; Commanding Officer's Quarters, 1963; Palisado Building Kitchen/Mess Room, 1963; Staff Officers' Quarters, 1990; Fort Clark Post Theater, 1997; Adjutant's Quarters (Quarters No. 20), 1999; Married Officers' Quarters 8–9, 2006; Officers' Quarters 2–3 and 4, 2007; U.S. Army Signal Corps Building, 2008; Army Service Club, 2009; New Cavalry Barracks, 2009; 1873 Infantry Barracks, 2010; Officers' Club Open-Mess, 2010; and 1886 Kitchen/Mess Hall, 2015) and, for eight sets of two-story stone officers' quarters built in 1873–74, the distinction of being the first Recorded Texas Historic Landmark District designated in Texas (Officers' Row Quarters, 1991).

In the ridiculously farcical book *The Lonely Sentinel*, an entirely fictional Lieutenant Sells of California is ordered to build a fort and build it to last. Of course, no officer named Sells ever served at Fort Clark, and no one ever received any such instructions. However, there is no doubt Fort Clark was built to last, as evidenced by the presence of log buildings now going on 170 years old and scores of stone buildings whose age is not far behind, the majority still in use for their original intended purpose.

Over the past thirty years, I have had the good fortune to be successful in submitting applications resulting in the award of fourteen of the twenty-one official Texas Historical Markers now on the grounds. Credit goes to Don Swanson (two), Ben Pingenot (two), B. Peter Pohl (two) and the Brackettville High School History Club (one) for the remaining seven. As the reader will discover, there are still over two dozen remaining U.S. Army buildings and features eligible for formal recognition. I am sharing my in-depth research and extensive image collection of these buildings in the hope of furthering interest in Fort Clark's military architecture while encouraging visitation to the Fort Clark Historic District. Many a visitor has uttered the now familiar comment, "There's a lot of history here!" To be certain, there is, just waiting to be discovered by residents and the traveling public seeking an unrivaled heritage tourism experience.

In the quiet time between the World Wars when an officer would find himself newly assigned to Fort Clark, Texas, he would most likely consult a popular reference book, *Army Posts & Towns: The Baedeker of the Army*. Here he could learn what to expect at his new duty station:

> *QUARTERS: Married Officers—There are 45 old, stone and wooden sets, all modernized, using Army ranges and heated by fireplaces and stoves. Bachelors—There are 2 buildings, 1 of stone and 1 of wood in which bachelors are quartered. There are 14 two-room suites. Warrant Officers—There are no quarters so designated, but warrant officers are assigned to available officers' quarters. Married N.C.O.'s—There are 45 old wood and stone sets, partially modernized, using coal ranges and heated by stoves. Fort Clark, although isolated from any large city, is considered by cavalrymen as a desirable station. It is famous for its wonderful springs of drinking water, its beautiful bridle paths, and its shady groves of forest monarchs many centuries old.*

OVERVIEW

The National Register Historic District

*The Fort Clark Historic District remains one of the most remarkably intact
districts entered into the National Register of Historic Places. The historic
integrity of the buildings and site is strong.*
—*Killis P. Almond Jr., preservation architect*

The Fort Clark Historic District was nominated to the National Register
by the Texas Historical Commission. The United States Department of
the Interior subsequently judged the district to possess a national level
of historic and architectural significance, entering it in the National Register
of Historic Places on December 6, 1979. Containing some sixty-five historic
U.S. Army structures, it ranks as the largest and most complete military
historic district under private ownership in the state of Texas and possibly
in the United States.

As a historic district, it is a geographically definable area with significant
linkage or continuity of sites, buildings, etc. that are historically related. The
National Park Service defines the National Register of Historic Places as

*a comprehensive catalog of our nation's cultural resources. It is our nation's
official acknowledgement, its honor roll, of properties significant in
American history, architecture, and archeology. Properties of state and local
as well as national significance are listed. Compositely, listed properties
provide a comprehensive index of the diversity of our American Heritage. It
is a record of the tangible elements of our past, a continuing inventory which*

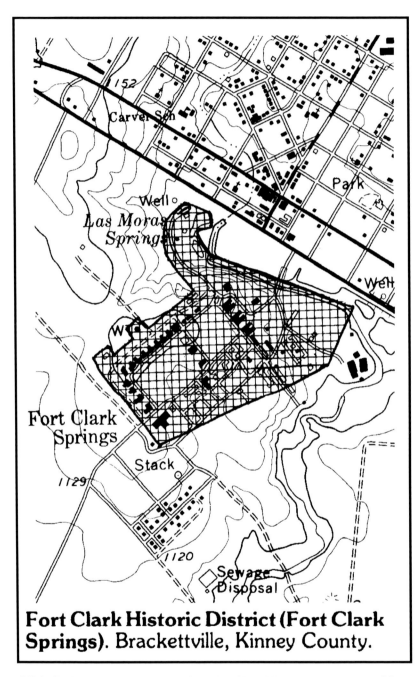

Fort Clark Historic District (Fort Clark Springs). Brackettville, Kinney County.

Official National Park Service map of the Fort Clark Historic District, 1979. *NPS.*

identifies both sites and material remains of the cultural developments that have molded the nation. As a list of significant sites and structures, the National Register also acts as an authoritative guide for assisting federal, state, and local governments, as well as private groups and citizens, to identify quickly the exact locations of historic resources.

The National Register narrative for the Fort Clark Historic District acknowledges,

Although construction of the fort spanned a period of approximately sixty years, the structures comprising the main body of the complex are integrally related to one another and the parade ground, and appear as components of a whole rather than individuals. While designs vary, characteristics common to all contribute significantly to the cohesion of the group. Solidly massed in simple geometric configuration, the one and two story buildings are constructed of native limestone obtained from fort property. They are sturdily built for function and endurance with a minimum of applied decorative. The structures comprising the Fort Clark Historic District reflect ninety-four years of continuous use as a military outpost. Primarily built by enlisted men using locally available materials, the buildings, constructed over a broad spectrum of time, reflect not only the changing needs of the military, but also the changing construction materials and techniques employed by the builders. Simple stone and wood structures arranged in a typical military complex layout were designed in relation to functional requirements. The existing compatibility is a result of the buildings' unified scale, materials, and massing and creates a rough, yet pleasing, landscape.

It must be pointed out, and any researcher cautioned, that the published National Register narrative and accompanying structure inventory for the district is an errata sheet nightmare. An astonishing 88 percent of the dating of structures is incorrect, including the misdating of seven buildings with cornerstones. Several dates are even in the wrong century. Two army-built historic facilities, the 1919 Water Power Plant and the 1925 Tennis Court, are given the status of "intrusions," and the distinction between "contributing" and "compatible" appears to be inconsistently and unfairly applied. The sheer number of errors is overwhelming. My efforts over the years to correct these unfortunate mistakes, following NPS guidelines, have failed to receive any response or positive result.

The initiative to seek recognition in the National Register originated with Nat Mendelsohn, president of North American Towns of Texas and purchaser of the fort grounds from the Brown Foundation in May 1971. The National Register of Historic Places Inventory—Nomination Form for the Fort Clark Historic District shows a "Historic Sites Inventory" was performed by the Texas Historical Commission in June 1976. At that time, only three structures had been previously recognized by the Texas Historical Commission and awarded State Historical Survey Committee Medallions in the 1960s, during the Guest Ranch era: the Guardhouse, the Wainwright House and the Palisado Building. All the medallions subsequently disappeared. These three, in addition to twenty-eight other properties, have since been designated Recorded Texas Historic Landmarks (RTHL). This status is only awarded to structures deemed worthy of preservation for their architectural integrity and historical associations and is the highest honor Texas bestows on the state's historic structures. Nearly thirty other properties remain to be recognized.

The Fort Clark Historic District is located in the southwest portion of central Texas near the center of Kinney County. Brackettville, the county seat, lies just outside the main gate on the north side. Geographically, the Fort Clark Historic District is situated several miles below the Balcones Escarpment, which separates the Edward's Plateau of the north central plains from the Rio Grande Plain. The district occupies a limestone ridge embraced in a curve of Las Moras Creek. Las Moras Spring lies within the district and produces approximately six million gallons a day, constituting the headwaters of the creek.

Fort Clark was established on June 20, 1852, when Companies C and E of the 1st Infantry commanded by Major Joseph H. LaMotte and an advance guard from the Regiment of Mounted Rifles occupied the site. The post was originally named Fort Riley, but its name was changed to Fort Clark on July 15, 1852, to honor a deceased officer of the 1st Infantry Regiment, Major John B. Clark, who had died of disease during the war with Mexico. The U.S. government formally leased the land for fifty dollars a month on July 30, 1852, from Samuel A. Maverick for a period not to exceed twenty years. In the same year, Oscar B. Brackett established a supply and stage stop outside the fort's northern boundary on the busy San Antonio/El Paso Military Road. Mary Maverick subsequently sold the four-thousand-acre tract to the United States of America for $60,000 in 1883.

As with other military posts on the Texas frontier, the building and ensuing growth of Fort Clark was driven by the needs of the army and the availability of soldier/civilian labor, accessibility of local building materials and government funding. The fort was abandoned on the eve of the Civil War and not reoccupied by federal forces until December 1866, when Fort Clark resumed its role as the southern anchor for the defense of the western frontier in Texas, the U.S. border with Mexico and the protection of the San Antonio/El Paso Military Road. The location of Fort Clark proved of strategic value because of the nearby eastern branch of the Great Comanche War Trail leading from the Central Plains into Mexico.

The greatest growth of Fort Clark and prosperity for Brackettville occurred during the First and Second World Wars, when the fort grew to accommodate first a medical division and finally a cavalry division of nearly ten thousand soldiers. Hundreds of temporary wood frame buildings were constructed, along with twenty-two additional permanent stone structures. When the post was closed following the end of World War II, the War Assets Administration through the Federal Works Agency sold the grounds, in 1946, to the highest bidder, the Texas Railway Equipment Company, for $411,250. The temporary frame structures and associated infrastructure were promptly demolished and sold for salvage. For the next generation, the property was operated as the Fort Clark Guest Ranch, until May 1971, when North American Towns of Texas Inc. purchased the site for $1 million and began developing a retirement/resort community and property owners' association, which operates today as the Fort Clark Springs Association.

Historic district structures by decade of construction. *Chart by author.*

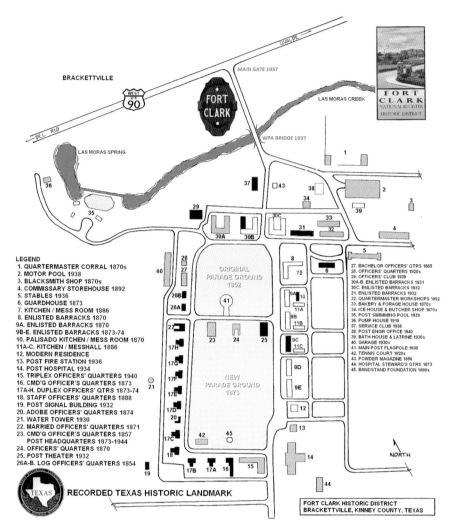

LEGEND
1. QUARTERMASTER CORRAL 1870s
2. MOTOR POOL 1938
3. BLACKSMITH SHOP 1870s
4. COMMISSARY STOREHOUSE 1892
5. STABLES 1936
6. GUARDHOUSE 1873
7. KITCHEN / MESS ROOM 1886
8. ENLISTED BARRACKS 1870
9A. ENLISTED BARRACKS 1870
9B-E. ENLISTED BARRACKS 1873-74
10. PALISADO KITCHEN / MESS ROOM 1870
11A-C. KITCHEN / MESSHALL 1886
12. MODERN RESIDENCE
13. POST FIRE STATION 1936
14. POST HOSPITAL 1934
15. TRIPLEX OFFICERS' QUARTERS 1940
16. CMD'G OFFICER'S QUARTERS 1873
17A-H. DUPLEX OFFICERS' QTRS 1873-74
18. STAFF OFFICERS' QUARTERS 1888
19. POST SIGNAL BUILDING 1932
20. ADOBE OFFICERS' QUARTERS 1874
21. WATER TOWER 1930
22. MARRIED OFFICERS' QUARTERS 1871
23. CMD'G OFFICER'S QUARTERS 1857
      POST HEADQUARTERS 1873-1944
24. OFFICERS' QUARTERS 1870
25. POST THEATER 1932
26A-B. LOG OFFICERS' QUARTERS 1854

27. BACHELOR OFFICERS' QTRS 1885
28. OFFICERS' QUARTERS 1920s
29. OFFICERS' CLUB 1939
30A-B. ENLISTED BARRACKS 1931
30C. ENLISTED BARRACKS 1932
31. ENLISTED BARRACKS 1932
32. QUARTERMASTER WORKSHOPS 1892
33. BAKERY & FORAGE HOUSE 1870s
34. ICE HOUSE & BUTCHER SHOP 1870s
35. POST SWIMMING POOL 1939
36. PUMP HOUSE 1919
37. SERVICE CLUB 1938
38. POST ENGR OFFICE 1940
39. BATH HOUSE & LATRINE 1930s
40. GARAGE 1930s
41. MAIN POST FLAGPOLE 1930
42. TENNIS COURT 1920s
43. POWDER MAGAZINE 1856
44. HOSPITAL STEWARD'S QTRS 1873
45. BANDSTAND FOUNDATION 1880s

RECORDED TEXAS HISTORIC LANDMARK

FORT CLARK HISTORIC DISTRICT
BRACKETTVILLE, KINNEY COUNTY, TEXAS

Site map of the Fort Clark National Register Historic District with designated Recorded Texas Historic Landmark properties in black and candidate properties in gray. *Map by the author.*

In 1981, the fledgling Fort Clark Historical Society was the recipient of a Survey and Planning Grant-in-Aid from the Department of the Interior, Heritage Conservation and Recreation Service. The grant was administered by the Texas Historical Commission under the provisions of the National Register Act of 1966. With matching private funds from Nathan (Nat) K. Mendelsohn, president, North American Towns of Texas Inc., a formal detailed preservation plan for the Fort Clark Historic District was prepared by a team of professional preservation architects and presented to the Fort Clark Springs Association Board of Directors. Although approved and adopted, sadly, the Preservation Plan, after the passage of over forty years, has yet to be implemented.

Recorded Texas Historic Landmarks are presented with a present-day image of the property along with the Texas Historical Marker inscription, followed by historic detail drawn from the narrative of the Texas Historical Marker application. Also presented are period maps and historic views of each structure. Many of the period photographs were taken by Carl Ekmark during his visit to the post on Wednesday, June 8, 1938. Several chapters include the Quartermaster drawings, plans and specifications and construction cost, if known. Extracts from the primary sources of the Inspection Report of 1928 and Killis P. Almond Jr.'s 1981 Preservation Plan are found throughout. Quotes from diaries, letters and memoirs reveal the lives and times of the buildings' occupants. Also highlighted are other historical markers in the district, along with buildings and sites not yet formally recognized for their historic contributions and associations.

The reader whose interest and curiosity are stimulated by this narrative is encouraged to consult Arcadia Publishing's *Fort Clark and Brackettville, Land of Heroes* (Images of America series) for dozens of additional images and further rich historic details. Inevitably, a visit to Fort Clark would also be in order.

PART I

THE NINETEENTH CENTURY

1855

ANTEBELLUM LOG OFFICERS' QUARTERS

Quarters No. 4 is on the left and Quarters No. 2–3 on the right in this modern view. *Photo by author.*

OFFICERS' QUARTERS 2–3 AND 4

THESE TWO BUILDINGS DATE FROM 1854–55, SOON AFTER THE U.S. ARMY ESTABLISHED FORT CLARK. THE ANTEBELLUM FORT THEN INCLUDED OFFICERS QUARTERS AND BARRACKS FOR ENLISTED MEN, AS WELL AS A TWO-STORY QUARTERMASTER STOREHOUSE, POWDER MAGAZINE, HOSPITAL, GUARDHOUSE AND POST HEADQUARTERS AROUND A PARADE GROUND. DURING THIS PERIOD, SUCH NOTABLE ARMY OFFICERS AS JOHN BELL HOOD, J.E.B. STUART, FITZHUGH LEE AND JAMES LONGSTREET SERVED HERE AND LIKELY LIVED IN THESE QUARTERS. HORIZONTAL LOGS AND VERTICAL POSTS WERE NOTCHED AND INTERLOCKED TO CREATE THESE BUILDINGS. LIMESTONE CHIMNEYS ARE ALSO HISTORIC. THE ARMY CLOSED THE FORT IN 1944, BY WHICH TIME THE BUILDINGS WERE CLAD IN LATH AND PLASTER AND WOOD SIDING.

—RHTL, 2007

Earliest known photograph of Quarters No. 2–3 and 4 (*right, foreground*) circa 1874. *Author's collection.*

Quarters No. 2–3 and Quarters No. 4 were uniquely constructed of vertical posts and horizontal logs in 1854–55 by the United States Army and were the first permanent quarters for officers built on Fort Clark. Today, these quarters continue to fulfill their original intended purpose of family housing and are the oldest extant structures in the Fort Clark Historic District.

Killis P. Almond Jr. noted in his 1981 Fort Clark Historic District Preservation Plan,

> *Horizontal log construction, notched and interlocked at the corners, is not a prevalent technique found along the Rio Grande because of the general unsuitability of sufficient timber reserves. There is horizontal log construction in the District, however, and it is unusual not only for the Rio Grande area but, also for this area of the United States. The method found here is indigenous to French Canadian log construction and is known as pièce sur pièce. This method consists of horizontal logs mortised into channels in upright corner posts and pegged securely in place.*

Almond further established,

> *These two buildings are one story and appear to have evolved similarly to one another. The end results differ slightly, but the overall configuration remains the same for both. These are the two buildings which are believed*

to be of vertical [horizontal] *log construction (pièce sur pièce) with adobe and/or stone and wood frame adjoining construction.*

When Fort Clark was established, there were sufficient wood reserves of live oak and cedar along Las Moras Creek and its environs to support the building of both picket and log buildings to serve as initial shelter for the garrison. Author of *Army Architecture in the West: Forts Laramie, Bridger, and D. A. Russell, 1849–1912* Alison K. Hoagland notes,

> *The army, like others establishing settlements in remote regions, favored log construction; at its most basic level, this required no sawmill but only an axe. For construction in quantity, the army was forced to adopt the more expeditious system of panel construction, which involved horizontal logs laid in between hewn vertical posts. The most likely source of panel construction was French Canada, where the technique called pièce sur pièce was used commonly.*

The antebellum fort consisted of three sets of officers' quarters made of log, a stone powder magazine, a two-story quartermaster storehouse, a stone hospital and a stone guard house, log barracks and a post headquarters building put up in 1857, which featured expert stone craftsmanship. During this period before the Civil War, such notable officers as John Bell Hood, J.E.B. Stuart and Fitzhugh Lee served at Fort Clark and may have lived in these log quarters. In 1854, then 2nd Lieutenant Zenas R. Bliss delivered a group of recruits from Fort Duncan to Fort Clark. That night, he "occupied a room with Lt. Otis, the first room belonging to government that I ever slept in." Returning to Fort Clark in 1885, as the lieutenant colonel of the 19th Infantry, Bliss was amazed that not only were these log quarters still standing, but they were also still in use. One of the earliest official observations of the log officers' quarters was made by Colonel Joseph K.F. Mansfield during his inspection of Fort Clark in December 1860. Colonel Mansfield noted on his map, "Old officers quarters of logs …These Buildings are of no value."

On July 20, 1870, Acting Assistant Surgeon Donald Jackson, United States Army, made the following report from Fort Clark on Quarters No. 2–3 and Quarters No. 4, at the time only about fifteen years old:

> *There are five buildings at present used as officers' quarters; three on the northwest side, framed, grass covered, square or gabled-roofed buildings. The space between the posts of the frame are filled with light logs, lying*

horizontally, and fitted into grooves in the post, they were put up in 1854–
55, and are 18 by 50 by 10 feet. In each end is a room, 18 by 20 feet, with
fireplace, two windows, and a door opening into a hall between these rooms,
which is open, except in one of these buildings; there are also dilapidated
portions of porches in front, and old stockade kitchens in the rear. All the
kitchens are shingled. These buildings are all leaky and generally in very
bad condition.

Quartermaster Department Form 3-24, "Description of Post of Fort Clark, Texas in 1901" describes Quarters 2–3 and 4 as being built of logs and in poor condition. The remarks state these quarters are old and unsuitable for officers and recommend they should be torn down and quarters for noncommissioned officer staff erected on the site.

Perhaps the most eminent occupant of these quarters was Hugh S. Johnson, United States Military Academy (USMA) class of 1903, who was a lieutenant in the 1st Cavalry at Fort Clark: "I lived in one of the oldest adobe houses, built eighty years ago. Indeed there were only a few modern quarters there."

Later a general officer, in 1933, Johnson was selected by President Roosevelt to head the National Recovery Administration, and in that position, he was named Time Magazine's Man of the Year for 1933.

During the Guest Ranch period, 1948–71, these two buildings were popular rentals and referred to as the Early American Cottages. Although today both buildings are stuccoed and altered, making documentation difficult without destructive techniques, the nineteenth-century maps of Fort Clark consistently identify Quarters No. 2–3 and Quarters No. 4 as being log structures. Thus, it stands to reason that during the nineteenth century, the logs were exposed. Conclusive evidence was established in 1996 when the current owner of Quarters No. 4 repaired the exterior plaster and lathe, revealing the original panel construction involving horizontal logs (some still with the bark on) mortised into six-inch square vertical posts. Additionally, during a recent renovation of Quarters No. 2–3, interior partition walls were also found to be horizontal log and vertical post construction, thus confirming Killis Almond's opinion that the pièce sur pièce technique was used for both buildings.

Remarkably, Quarters No. 2–3 and Quarters No. 4 have maintained their architectural integrity as the only log officer's quarters remaining in the district, surviving multiple recommendations to be "torn down" and withstanding the ravages of time for nearly 170 years. Throughout their

Exposed log pièce sur pièce construction, Quarters No. 4. *Photo by author.*

Notched logs with the bark still present from an interior wall of Quarters 2–3, cut in 1854. *Photo by author.*

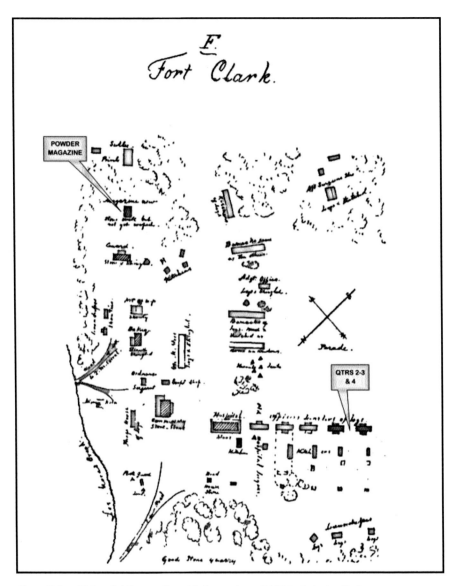

Above: Colonel Mansfield's map from his inspection of 1856. *Author's collection.*

Opposite, top: Carl Ekmark image, Quarters No. 4, Wednesday, June 8, 1938. *Author's collection.*

Opposite, bottom: Carl Ekmark image, Quarters No. 2–3, Wednesday, June 8, 1938. *Author's collection.*

existence, these sturdy log structures have proven to be exceptionally well made and retained their individuality and unique character next to their larger, more imposing stone neighbors. They are quite possibly the sole remaining examples of this type of military architecture in Texas or the nation.

1870

PALISADO BUILDING KITCHEN/MESS ROOM

Palisado Building Kitchen/Mess Room today. *Photo by author.*

PALISADO BUILDING KITCHEN / MESS ROOM
THIS STRUCTURE WAS BUILT BY THE U.S. ARMY IN 1869–70 AND IS AN EXAMPLE
OF VERTICAL POST OR JACAL CONSTRUCTION, USED DUE TO THE ABSENCE OF
TREES TALL ENOUGH FOR TRADITIONAL HORIZONTAL LOG CONSTRUCTION.
AFRICAN AMERICAN "BUFFALO SOLDIERS" OF THE 25TH INFANTRY BUILT THE
RECTANGULAR PLAN STRUCTURE WITH WOOD SHINGLE ROOF FOR USE AS A
MESS ROOM LOCATED BEHIND THEIR NEW STONE BARRACKS. THE BUILDING
WAS LATER A COMPANY STOREROOM, TAILOR SHOP AND AMUSEMENT HALL.
SOME SOURCES MISTAKENLY IDENTIFIED THIS BUILDING AS THE "ROBERT E.
LEE BUILDING," EVEN THOUGH LEE NEVER VISITED FORT CLARK WHILE HE WAS
IN TEXAS.
—RTHL, 1963

The Palisado Building Kitchen/Mess room was built by the United States Army in 1869 and is the only remaining vertical log constructed (cedar post) or jacal building in the district. Today, the building is still in use as a meeting place and is one of Fort Clark's most iconic structures. Within its walls, men who fought at Gettysburg, the Little Big Horn, San Juan Hill and Château Thierry shared meals and told their stories of soldiering.

Many of Fort Clark's early buildings used the practical construction technique of vertical posts, which was a typical frontier military expedient in Texas. Trees were simply not tall enough to allow for traditional log cabin construction. These often drafty and critter-infested structures were a common source of complaints by army wives, contributing to the "glittering misery" of antebellum garrison life on the fort. In her 1893 book *I Married a Soldier*, Lydia Spencer Lane, wife of Lieutenant William Bartlett Lane of the Mounted Rifles, described her quarters at Fort Clark in 1855:

> *A funny little house had been put up for us before we arrived, all the quarters for officers being occupied. The walls were built of green logs with the bark left on them, and they were set up on end, not like the usual log cabin. The Mexicans call a house of this kind a "jacal." The walls were seven or eight feet high, and supported a slanting roof. There was really but one room in the house, with an enormous chimney, built of stone, in the middle of it. The spaces between the logs were chinked with mud, or plaster, perhaps, but that was all the plaster there was about it. We had no ceiling, nothing but the shingles over our heads through the long, hot summer. On one side of the big chimney was the bedroom, on the other, a sitting room.*

The Palisado building was erected in 1869–70, by the Buffalo Soldiers of the 25th Infantry, to serve as a mess room behind their new stone barracks. The first detailed description of the building is found in War Department Surgeon General's Office Circular No. 4, *Report on Barracks and Hospitals with Descriptions of Military Posts*, by John S. Billings, assistant surgeon, United States Army:

The report of Acting Assistant Surgeon Donald Jackson, U.S. Army, July 20, 1870, describes the building as follows:

> *A kitchen and mess-room of stockade, and shingled, has been erected for one of the barracks; it is in the rear of and parallel to the latter; has one double door and three windows in front, and one door in the rear, with fireplace in one end; it has no fixtures as yet.*

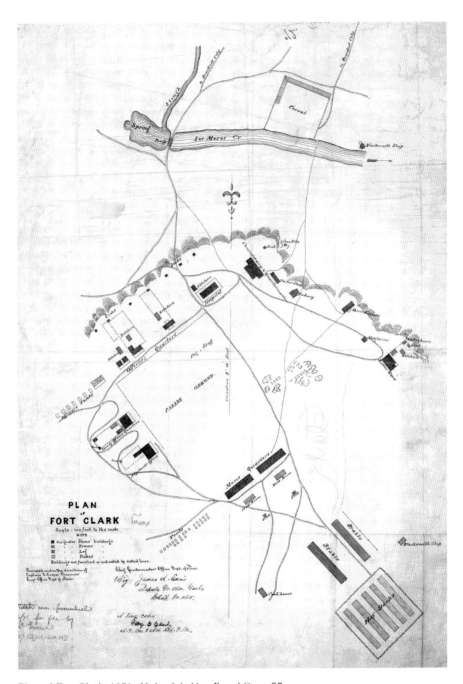

Plan of Fort Clark, 1871. *National Archives Record Group 77.*

Despite its primitive architecture, the building proved durable and of considerable utility during its seventy-five years of military service, having seen use primarily as a kitchen/mess room and in turn as a company storeroom, tailor shop, and then as an amusement hall at the end of the nineteenth century. A unique feature of the building is that the interior walls are lined with tin. This treatment employs flattened fuel cans as a wall covering, which keeps the building comfortable in all seasons.

During the Guest Ranch era, the new civilian owners of Fort Clark continued to mistakenly identify this building as the "Robert E. Lee Headquarters," as the army had done before them. It is a certain historic fact that Robert E. Lee never visited or served at Fort Clark during his pre–Civil War service with the 2nd Cavalry in Texas, from March 1856 to October 1857 and again from February 1860 to February 1861. Lee never returned to Texas and died in Virginia in October 1870, the same year the Palisado Building was constructed. The origins of this unfortunate and persistent myth can be traced to the U.S. Army's own shoddy history of Fort Clark. Lee's acclaimed biographer, Douglas Southall Freeman, in his Pulitzer Prize–winning work *R.E. Lee: A Biography*, meticulously chronicles the activities, itineraries and whereabouts of Lee while he was in Texas, using Lee's personal and official correspondence; there is no mention of Fort Clark. There is also no record of Lee to be found in Fort Clark's post returns. Yet despite the irrefutable documentation, Lee's well-deserved fame as an American military hero figure has left behind more than a few

World War II–era real picture postcard (RPPC) of the Palisado Building. *Author's collection.*

R.L. Warren 1950s Guest Ranch–era RPPC of the Palisado Building. *Author's collection.*

hoaxes from the historical license taken at several Texas sites never visited by Lee, similar to the mythical "Washington slept here" phenomenon prevalent to this day at false sites throughout the thirteen original colonies. Hopefully, the facts and thus the truth can now be known: Robert E. Lee never, ever, visited Fort Clark!

However, the authentic and proud history of the Palisado Building stands on its own merits, and the structure remains a genuine treasure of our community. In 1963, the building was awarded a State Historical Survey Committee Medallion by the Texas Historical Commission, which disappeared over time and has since been replaced by an official Texas Historical Marker. An extensive restoration and stabilization of the building was completed in 1994 by the Fort Clark Springs Association. The Fort Clark Historical Society now cares for the building and uses it as a meeting hall.

1871

MARRIED OFFICERS' QUARTERS 8–9

(AUTHOR'S HOME)

Married Officers' Quarters 8–9 today. *Photo by author.*

MARRIED OFFICERS' QUARTERS 8–9

THIS SINGLE-STORY DUPLEX ONCE SERVED AS HOUSING FOR MARRIED OFFICERS
AND THEIR FAMILIES AT FORT CLARK. THE U.S. ARMY FORT, ESTABLISHED
IN 1852 TO DEFEND THE WESTERN FRONTIER OF TEXAS AND THE BORDER
WITH MEXICO, SAW SIGNIFICANT GROWTH IN THE 1870s. TO ACCOMMODATE
A REGIMENTAL SIZE GARRISON, THE ARMY CONSTRUCTED LIVING QUARTERS
SUCH AS THIS PARTICULAR HOUSE. BUILT BY 1875 OUT OF UNCOURSED, ROUGH-
CUT LIMESTONE, THE BUILDING FEATURES A CROSS-HIPPED ROOF, INTERIOR
CHIMNEYS WITH DOUBLE FIREPLACES AND A DISTINCTIVE U-SHAPE. THE FORT
CLOSED IN 1944 AND LATER OWNERS TRANSFORMED THE QUARTERS INTO A
SINGLE FAMILY HOME.

—RTHL, 2006

Quarters Number 8–9 was built by the United States Army between 1871 and 1873. This single-story double set of quarters is constructed of local limestone and situated first in the line of company grade officer's quarters. Today, the property continues to fulfill its original intended purpose of family housing.

Killis Almond Jr. noted, "This one story building has an irregular plan with hipped and gabled roofs....The configuration now is basically a U with the courtyard at the rear formed between two wings."

In early summer of 1870, a single-story double set of stone officer's quarters was completed alongside the 1857 stone commanding officer's quarters. The report of Acting Assistant Surgeon Donald Jackson, United States Army, July 20, 1870, describes the building as follows:

> *On the southwest side of the rectangle are two stone buildings, with shingled roofs; one built in 1857, the other just completed; the latter, now occupied as headquarters, is intended for two sets of quarters—dimensions 50 by 37½ by 12 feet. It has two halls, 6 feet wide, through the center. The front room in each set is 18 by 18 feet; each has one fireplace, two windows in the front, and one in the end, and each communicates both with the hall and the room in the rear. The latter are not quite so large. In each there is also a fireplace and two windows, with door opening into the hall. From one side, or set of quarters in this building, there extends a stone building, shed roof, shingled, 36 by 12 feet, divided into three equal apartments, the one adjoining the main building communicating with it by a door and window; one used as dining-room, another as kitchen, and the third as servant's room. The new building* [later designated Quarters 6–7] *was designed for two sets of officers' quarters. The set with the dining-room, kitchen, and servant's room is at present occupied by the commanding officer. The double hall style of building, like the new quarters, is not well adapted for this climate, as the wind in the warm season invariably blows from the same direction, southeast or east; unless the building fronts toward the east or southeast, one set of quarters must effectually shut off from the direct breeze.*

As Quarters 8–9 has virtually the identical floor plan and dimensions, the description is, for all intents and purposes, also the basic plan for Quarters 8–9.

The first map to show a structure in the space now occupied by Quarters 8–9 is a sketch dated June 26, 1871 (see page 37). The then frame building faces southeast, with a porch across the front. A line of officer's tents extends to the southwest, where the "new post" would be laid out just two years later, in 1873.

By 1874, Fort Clark had grown to accommodate and support the regimental-size garrison needed to deal effectively with the increasing number of Indian depredations along the border. The post doubled in size from 1873 to 1875. Quarters 8–9 next appears on the map of Fort Clark in the "Outline Description of the Military Posts in the Division of the Missouri" dated April 15, 1876. This reference also states, "Officers' quarters, twenty sets built of stone [eight two-story duplexes and two one-story double sets, No. 6–7 and No. 8–9] and one built of adobe [No. 20]." Quarters 8–9 is no longer frame but now stone, with two wings.

Stone is the predominant construction material used within the district, and Quarters 8–9 is a solid case in point. The use of stone comprised a variety of techniques, which can be divided into two basic areas. The first encompasses the years 1870 to 1910, when stone was used in load-bearing masonry walls and foundations, as in the Quarters 8–9 pier and beam foundation. The stone was taken from a local quarry, which remains today. It was most often laid up as coursed rubble, and the surfacing was common faced. Decorative work, aside from surfacing treatments, is minimal. The windows and doors of Quarters 8–9 are predominately spanned with solid timbers.

Maps of the post and comparative analysis of period photographs reflect little change to the appearance of Quarters No. 8–9 well into the early twentieth century. Panoramic photos circa 1925 and 1939 clearly show the space between the wings to be covered, adding to the living area, and wood additions on the end of each wing.

As the National Register narrative notes, "Twentieth century construction on the fort continued to acknowledge the abundance of locally available stone, although the method of construction varied from that of the earlier buildings." Sometime between 1932 and 1938, a fourteen-by-thirty-seven-foot addition was added to Quarters No. 8. This addition to the east side of the building is built of tile brick veneered with an irregular cut fieldstone and a plain mortar joint. It contains two bedrooms separated by a common bathroom. The addition may have been a necessity to provide much-needed additional living space for an officer with a large family. Quarters No. 9 remained unchanged during this period.

In the *Report of Inspection of Buildings and Utilities at Fort Clark, Texas*, conducted from October 17 to 20, 1928, and published by the Office of the

Quartermaster, Headquarters 8th Corps Area, Fort Sam Houston, Texas, a detailed description of Quarters No. 8 and 9 was made, as follows:

Building Number 8 and 9

> *8 and 9—Married Officers' Quarters—double set.*
>   *Construction—one story stone*
>   *Foundation—rock*
>   *Roof—asbestos shingles*
>   *Floors—wood*
>   *Dimensions—52' x 86'*
>
>   *Apply two coats of paint to exterior woodwork.*
>   *Rehang two exterior screen doors.*
>   *Repair two front screen doors.*
>   *Replace floor of front porch with concrete.*
>   *Provide concrete curb and bases for porch rail and columns.*
>   *Repair porch railing—requiring 8 pieces, 2" x 4" x 12'*
>   *Reputty 50 window panes, 7" x 12"*
>   *Rebuild one kitchen chimney.*
>
> *Interior of No. 8*
>   *Replace 3 transom glass 12" x 14"*
>   *Replace 220' of flooring in sitting room.*
>   *Replace 100' of flooring in kitchen.*
>   *Apply one coat of calzimine to walls throughout.*
>   *Apply one coat of paint to bathroom.*
>
> *Interior of No. 9*
>   *Rebuild decaying boards in wall partition between kitchen and dining room.*
>   *Provide one new 2'8" x 6'8" panel door with frame.*
>   *Repair plaster in kitchen around conduit entrance.*
>   *Provide new 2'8" x 6'8" panel door to dining room.*
>   *Replace 60 brick in fireplace.*
>   *Apply one coat of paint to bathroom and kitchen.*
>   *Apply one coat of calzimine to walls throughout.*
>   *Dining room table consists of 6" tongue and groove floor material and is wholly unsuitable for such a purpose.*

Officers and ladies in front of Quarters No. 8–9, circa 1902. *Author's collection.*

Lippe Studios of Del Rio postcard, 1930s. *Author's collection.*

Carl Ekmark image, Quarters No. 8–9, Wednesday, June 8, 1938. *Author's collection.*

W.M. Cline RPPC, 1950s view, during the Guest Ranch era, then the home of Slim and Olla Belle Dahlstrom. *Author's collection.*

During the Guest Ranch period, 1948–71, Quarters No. 8–9 was the vacation home retreat of Frederick L. "Slim" Dahlstrom, owner of the Texas Railway Equipment Company, and his wife, Olla Belle, who transformed the duplex into its present configuration as a spacious single-family home by means of two doorways cut along the centerline of the building joining the two sets of quarters. Of note are two subsequent owners of the property: Minot Tully Pratt Jr., general manager of the Aircraft Conversion Co. and legendary racecar driver A.J. Foyt Jr. Quarters No. 8–9 maintains its architectural integrity as one of only two single-story stone double sets of officer's quarters in the Historic District, while standing the test of time for over 150 years since 1871.

1873

COMMANDING OFFICER'S QUARTERS

(WAINWRIGHT HOUSE)

The Wainwright House today. *Photo by author.*

COMMANDING OFFICER'S QUARTERS

FORT CLARK WAS ESTABLISHED AS A U.S. ARMY GARRISON IN JUNE 1852. NINE STRUCTURES DESIGNED BY U.S. ARMY ENGINEERS WERE BUILT IN 1873–1874 TO HOUSE THE FORT'S OFFICERS. THIS HOUSE SERVED THE FORT'S COMMANDING OFFICERS, INCLUDING COL. RANALD S. MACKENZIE AND GEN. JONATHAN M. WAINWRIGHT. ARCHITECTURAL FEATURES INCLUDE A CENTRAL ENTRY, WOOD-FRAME PORCH, SIX-OVER-SIX WINDOWS, SECOND FLOOR DORMERS, AND FOUR LARGE CHIMNEYS WITH SCULPTED CAPS.

—RTHL, 1963

The Commanding Officer's Quarters was built by the United States Army during the spring and early summer of 1873 of local limestone at a cost of $6,613.11 and is a contributing structure to the National Register Historic District. It remains the only surviving example in the nation of Quartermaster General Montgomery Meigs's Model Plan No. 4 of 1872. Today, the property continues to fulfill its original intended purpose of providing family housing. This imposing residence is an enduring element of the landscape of Fort Clark and commands the parade ground today as the home's notable occupants did in years past.

On January 2, 1873, Inspector General Colonel Edmund Schriver (USMA 1833, Brevet Major General) arrived at Fort Clark to inspect the post. A full thirteen years had passed since the fort was last inspected, on the eve of the Civil War in 1860. Colonel Schriver found the soldiers' quarters to be "wretchedly constructed" and all but two companies living in huts. He further remarked on the "utter inadequacy of decent quarters for officers." However, he noted, two new barracks were in progress and new stables were being constructed on a "good plan." The commander of the Department of Texas, Brigadier General C.C. Augur, visited the post the next month, perhaps to confirm Colonel Schriver's observations. In April, the post was visited by Secretary of War William Belknap and General Philip H Sheridan. The post return for the same month makes the first mention of the garrison "assisting in building the new Post." The long-overdue permanent improvements to living conditions at Fort Clark had finally begun.

The number of civilians employed by the Quartermaster Department, specifically carpenters and masons, increased from just five in January 1873 to a high of forty-seven by July that year. It stands to reason that the new quarters for the commanding officer of the post was a priority. Also noteworthy during this period is that no quarrymen were employed, which would indicate the stone was not being obtained on the fort grounds.

The quarters of the commanding officer was always the finest home on a post. The floor plan of the first floor is of significance, as it contributed to the "society" of the post during the Victorian era. The parlor served as a room for receiving and entertaining visitors. In the frontier army of the late nineteenth century, having a parlor was evidence of social status— particularly, in this case, for the commanding officer of the post. It was proof that an officer had achieved rank and privilege above the junior officers, who often lived in only one or two rooms. As the parlor was the place where the larger world encountered the private sphere of army life, it was, as a rule, the most formal and finest room in the home. The parlor displayed a family's best furnishings and treasures, portraits of family members or senior officers of the army, hunting trophies, souvenirs of past service, works of art, books and other evidence of refinement and military achievement.

The first-floor front bedroom, no doubt, served as a sitting room. The sitting room provided a personal place for family only and was furnished with comfortable chairs and lounges for relaxing, offering escape from the tedium and responsibility of command. One might also find an assortment of wicker furniture, a mainstay and favorite of army families as it was inexpensive, lightweight and could survive many moves.

Almost certainly, second-floor bedrooms often served as accomodations for visiting senior officers. Fort Clark's post commanders were much older officers without small children and were able to set aside guest lodging for field grade and general officers temporarily at the post on official business, such as inspections, boards of inquiry and courts-martial duty. Perhaps the most distinguished visitor was General William Tecumseh Sherman, on his four-day visit to Fort Clark in March 1882. We can only imagine how many other prominent officers slept in these rooms.

It remains an army tradition to name the most important quarters on each post in honor of the highest-ranking officer to have resided within its walls. As a result, several posts have a Pershing House. However, only one post has a Wainwright House. These quarters were first occupied by Colonel Ranald S. Mackenzie, who, as a bachelor and workaholic, no

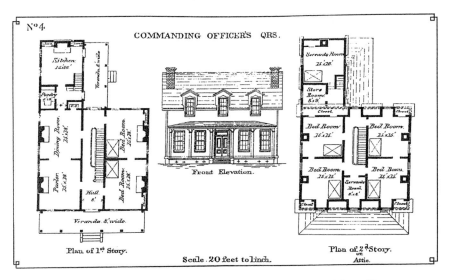

Quartermaster Department Model Plan No. 4. *National Archives Record Group 77.*

Family of Colonel Henry M. Lazelle (*right*), 18ᵗʰ Infantry, post commander 1889–94. *Courtesy James Carson.*

How many soldiers sent a postcard home of the Commanding Officer's Quarters? *Author's collection.*

doubt had little use for its six bedrooms. Another well-known occupant of the 1870s was William R. "Pecos Bill" Shafter. Throughout the remainder of the nineteenth century, the senior officer of the post, usually a colonel commanding a regiment, called these quarters home. It was indeed a privilege for junior officers, such as Lieutenant Francis H. French of the 19th Infantry, to be invited to dine with the colonel and his lady (then, in 1884, Brevet Major General and Medal of Honor recipient Charles H. Smith) in the grandest quarters on the post.

In 1923, these quarters were designated for the commanding officer of the 1st Cavalry Brigade, a brigadier general. It was in that assignment that Medal of Honor recipient Jonathan M. Wainwright—after an absence of some thirty years, having first served at Fort Clark with the 1st Cavalry from 1906 to 1908—returned to occupy these quarters with his wife, Kitty, from December 1938 until September 1940. Major General Harry H. Johnson, first cousin of President Lyndon Baines Johnson, lived here in 1943–44 while commanding the 2nd Cavalry Division. Not to be outdone by famous military men, Hollywood icon John Wayne selected this home as his residence during the making of his epic film *The Alamo* in 1959.

1873

1873 INFANTRY BARRACKS

Modern view of Fort Clark's infantry barracks. *Photo by author.*

1873 INFANTRY BARRACKS

FORT CLARK BY 1873 HAD GROWN TO REGIMENTAL SIZE, COMPELLING CONSTRUCTION OF SIX SINGLE-STORY INFANTRY BARRACKS AND THREE TWO-STORY CAVALRY BARRACKS BY THE U.S. ARMY QUARTERMASTER DEPARTMENT. THIS ONE-STORY RECTANGULAR PLAN BARRACKS WAS BUILT OF COURSED RUBBLE LIMESTONE WITH A GABLE WOOD SHINGLE ROOF, STONE FIREPLACES, CENTRAL ROOF VENT AND SHED FRONT PORCH. THE OPEN INTERIOR HOUSED BUNKS FOR SIXTY-FOUR SOLDIERS WITH A SINGLE GUN RACK IN THE CENTER OF THE OPEN BAY. THE COMPANY BARRACKS FACED THE OFFICERS' QUARTERS TO THE WEST ACROSS THE PARADE FIELD. TODAY THIS BUILDING IS THE BEST SURVIVING EXAMPLE OF ITS KIND AT FORT CLARK, AND ONE OF A HANDFUL OF INDIAN WARS PERIOD BARRACKS LEFT ON ANY POST IN THE NATION.

—RTHL, 2010

Fort Clark's only remaining essentially unaltered 1873 Infantry Barracks served as quarters for enlisted men of the fort's garrison for over seventy years, from 1873 to 1944. The building is recognized in the National Register narrative as a contributing structure to the Fort Clark Historic District. This distinctive building was home for generations of soldiers from the Indian Wars of the nineteenth century to World War II in the twentieth century.

As noted by Killis P. Almond Jr. in his 1981 Fort Clark Historic District Preservation Plan description of the six infantry barracks,

> *They were all originally constructed as company barracks and faced the officers' quarters to the west across the parade field. They were all one story rectangular plan barracks constructed of coursed rubble limestone with gable wood shingle roofs. Plain shed front (west) porches are typical as well as six over six wood sash windows and four panel wood doors.*

The earliest quarters for soldiers at Fort Clark were tents along Las Moras Creek near the spring. "The troops are in tents & the ground is such as to prevent their being encamped together, this dispersion is of course very unfavorable to discipline," wrote Lieutenant Colonel Joseph E. Johnston, 1st Cavalry, of his inspection of the post on November 9, 1859. One year later, in December 1860, Colonel Joseph K.F. Mansfield found little had changed, commenting,

> *"Yet it has improved less in accommodations for the military command than any post I have hitherto seen. While other posts have been built & rebuilt, this post has hardly progressed at all."*

Mansfield also reported that several companies were quartered in worthless temporary buildings of logs set in the ground and thatched, with earthen floors and neither fireplaces nor glass windows. He recommended new quarters of stone from the local quarry and a congressional appropriation of $15,000 for that purpose. Nothing came of Mansfield's advice, for when Federal troops surrendered the fort to Texas Confederates in March 1861, on the eve of the Civil War, they burned the wooden barracks then in use.

Not until 1870 did permanent quarters for soldiers exist on Fort Clark. Two single-story infantry barracks were built of stone that year by the Buffalo Soldiers of the 25th Infantry. By 1873, the fort's garrison had grown to regimental size, requiring the largest construction effort in the fort's existence. Four single-story infantry barracks and three two-story cavalry barracks, all of stone, were completed in 1873–74 by skilled civilian carpenters, masons and quarrymen employed by the Quartermaster Department.

The *Plan of Soldiers Barracks, Fort Clark, Texas* was prepared in the office of the chief quartermaster, Department of Texas, San Antonio, Texas, in August 1872; approved by Major General C.C. Augur, commander of the Department of Texas; and respectfully submitted to the Deputy Quartermaster General, United States Army, Lieutenant Colonel Samuel B. Holabird, who had served at Fort Clark as a lieutenant assigned to the 1st Infantry in 1858. The estimated cost was $3,601.76 per building. On September 26, 1872, the plan was approved by the Secretary of War, changing the stone foundations from three to two feet and omitting the corners. An order to Colonel Daniel H. Rucker, then Assistant Quartermaster General, included the note:

> *In original papers it is proposed to erect 5 such Buildings also 5 Bdgs for Officers Qtrs per plan attached—at a total cost of $31,665.55—under existing laws only $20,000 could be expended—which was authorized in money remitted to Col Rucker.*

Of the five proposed barracks, only four were built, undoubtedly due to the reduction in the appropriation. The plan called for a single-story building of stone, 111 x 27 feet with a 10-foot porch, enclosed 9 x 16½ foot frame rooms

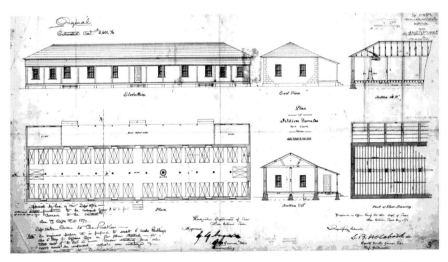

Quartermaster Department plan for soldier barracks at Fort Clark 1872. *National Archives Record Group 77.*

on each end of the porch and a hip roof. The quartermaster drawing also shows bunks for sixty-four soldiers and a single gun rack in the center of the open bay. There is no provision on the plan for heating or ventilation of the building, a source of considerable controversy between the Quartermaster Department and the Medical Department at the time. Modifications to approved Quartermaster Department plans were commonplace at western posts, and Fort Clark was no exception. Large stone fireplaces were added at each end of the barracks, along with a central roof vent. The interior support posts were eliminated and high vaulted ceilings substituted.

The only specific reference to and detailed description of this building (post building No. 37) is found on page 105 of the *Report of Inspection of Buildings and Utilities at Fort Clark, Texas*, conducted from October 17 to 20, 1928, and published by the Office of the Quartermaster, Headquarters 8th Corps Area, Fort Sam Houston, Texas:

Building Number 37

37—Troop Barracks: One story structure. Foundation, stone. Roof, wood shingles. Floors, wood. Dimensions 27' x 111'.
 Repair roof at end of porch, serving as barber shop.
 Repair flashing around two chimneys.
 Repoint cracks in stone wall over an area of 100 ft.
 Resurface six treads of steps at rear of building with concrete.
 Provide screened frames for four foundation vents.
 Paint exterior woodwork two coats in conformity with post color scheme.
 Replace three screen doors, 2'8" x 6'8"
 Replace 150 ft. of window screen.

Interior of No. 37
 Replace two panel door, 3' x 7'
 Replace 100 brick in fire places.
 Required, 500 ft. of flooring in front squad room.
 Repair two hearths with concrete, 4' x 7'.

Since 1873, the buildings have experienced alterations and remodeling to suit either the needs of the army or, now, the whims of private civilian owners. The first barracks in the line, built in 1870, took on an *L* shape sometime between 1873 and 1876, intended to provide additional space for soldiers and noncommissioned officers. Funding constraints prevented any such change to the other five barracks. In the mid-1930s, four of the barracks were connected in sets of two (barracks 2–3 and 5–6) with stone additions, leaving only this fourth barracks in the line unaltered. Civilian ownership after 1971 brought with it more historically destructive "remuddling," with the unsympathetic modification of rooflines adding dormers and half-stories. This leaves only this fourth barracks in the line as the best surviving example of the original soldiers' barracks plan of 1872 in the Fort Clark Historic District and perhaps the only one of its type in Texas.

This soldiers' barracks served the garrison for seventy-one years until Fort Clark's closure in 1944 and is a classic, enduring example of utilitarian U.S. Army architecture from the late nineteenth century, with a one-of-a-kind design suited to the needs of the expanding post garrison in the early 1870s.

During the Guest Ranch era, this barracks was transformed into an elegant, spacious home by George Brown, of Brown and Root, and used as his vacation retreat. Today, over 150 years later, the building continues to provide shelter and comfort as originally intended and is being responsibly maintained in a good state of repair by the current owners. Of the six single-story stone infantry soldier barracks in the Fort Clark Historic District, all but one have experienced irreversible unsympathetic modifications. Only this barracks stands out as basically unaltered and an exemplary model of preservation.

The 1873 Infantry Barracks is the finest example of nineteenth-century soldier housing remaining intact in the Fort Clark Historic District. This

Company of the 23rd Infantry formed in front of their barracks at Fort Clark, circa 1895. *Author's collection.*

Top: Rare view of the barracks room of Company D, 23rd Infantry at Fort Clark in January 1894, complete with idle soldiers, rifle rack and Model 1891 two-burner pendant barracks lamps. *Author's collection.*

Bottom: View of barracks, 1941, then occupied by a unit of the 112th Cavalry, Texas National Guard. The latrine at the end of the porch now has a rock veneer. *Author's collection.*

building may well be one of only a handful of Indian Wars–period single-story stone barracks left on any post in the nation and perhaps the sole original example of this type of military architecture still standing in Texas.

1874

OFFICERS' ROW QUARTERS

Officers' Row marker at Quarters No. 10–11. *Photo by author.*

OFFICERS' ROW QUARTERS

FORT CLARK WAS ESTABLISHED AS A U.S. ARMY GARRISON IN 1852. THE ORIGINAL QUARTERS WERE CRUDE LOG HUTS AND HOUSES OF PALISADE CONSTRUCTION. IN 1857, A NEW PROGRAM BEGAN TO REPLACE BADLY DILAPIDATED STRUCTURES WITH BUILDINGS OF QUARRIED STONE. DESIGNED AND CONSTRUCTED IN 1873–74 AS DUPLEXES TO ACCOMMODATE TWO OFFICERS' FAMILIES EACH, THESE EIGHT RESIDENCES CLOSELY RESEMBLE THOSE BUILT ON OTHER MILITARY POSTS DURING THAT TIME PERIOD. THE BUILDINGS REFLECT AN EVOLUTIONARY ADAPTATION OF MILITARY DESIGN SUITED TO LOCAL CONSTRUCTION MATERIALS AND THE REGIONAL CLIMATE. EACH DUPLEX HAS THREE LARGE ROOMS ON EACH FLOOR, TWO FIREPLACES AND A FIFTY-FIVE-FOOT FRONT PORCH. AN 1885 REMODELING PROJECT CHANGED THE HOUSES FROM RECTANGULAR TO T-PLAN. THE ARMY CONTRACTED WITH CENTRAL POWER AND LIGHT COMPANY FOR ELECTRICITY IN 1918. FORT CLARK WAS DEACTIVATED IN 1946 AND SOLD TO

THE BROWN AND ROOT CORPORATION. IN 1971, THE FORT PROPERTY BECAME "FORT CLARK SPRINGS," A PRIVATE RECREATIONAL COMMUNITY. THE OFFICERS' HOUSES WERE RENTED TO MEMBERS AND GUESTS UNTIL 1974, WHEN THEY WERE OFFERED FOR SALE TO MEMBERS OF THE FORT CLARK SPRINGS ASSOCIATION.

—RTHL, 1991

Unfortunately, this inscription uses the most inappropriate and inaccurate term *deactivated* to describe Fort Clark's retirement from active service. The U.S. Army reserves the term *deactivated* for explosive ordnance and units— never for posts, camps and stations. The correct, proper terminology is simply *closed*.

Built between September 1873 and August 1874 to U.S. Quartermaster Department plans and specifications, at a cost of $6,955.72 each, these eight double sets of officers' quarters have endured as sturdy, comfortable family housing for over 150 years. Each building is of a predominantly Georgian style, built as a double set of quarters, with the stair hall and kitchen wing of the two units sharing a common wall. This was, by and large, the most widespread plan used for officer quarters at frontier posts between 1866 and 1890. All are contributing structures to the district and, also, make up the only Recorded Texas Historic Landmark District in Texas. They stand today as the iconic sentinels of the parade ground. The National Register Narrative points out,

> Solid stone construction with less refinement was employed in many of the buildings erected during the 1860s and 1870s including the enlisted men and officers' quarters. The blocks have a more irregular shape, rougher surface, and less clearly defined edge than those used on the old Headquarters Building. In addition, the doors and windows feature wooden rather than stone lintels. Constructed along the west and south sides of the parade ground, the officers' quarters consist of two story structures made to accommodate two families each with identical floor plans on either side of a dividing wall. Large porches with diagonal enhance the front facades and dormer windows pierce the steep pitch gable roofs.

Killis P. Almond Jr.'s evaluation in 1981 observed,

> These one and one-half story stone buildings were constructed during the 1870s as officers' quarters to replace earlier adobe and log quarters. The "T" plan is typical, the cap of the "T" being the main body of the house

with the stem being a service area and servant's quarters. Each house consists of two units which are separated by a stone party wall. The front porch is a hipped roof which frames into the wall below four dormer windows which pierce the eave line. The cornice is carried up and over each dormer which forms a hood. The roofs are gabled and originally wood shingled. Windows are typically six-over-six, double hung wood sash with four panel wood doors. The stone masonry is coursed rubble with original pointing raised and struck. The condition of all the buildings is fairly good, but all have suffered the usual alterations, additions and cement pointing and parging.

By 1874, Fort Clark had its own lime kiln, sawmill and quarry. At the height of construction, in January and February 1874, the Quartermaster Department employed as many as 143 skilled civilian laborers, including 44 carpenters, 104 masons and 24 quarrymen. The February 1874 post return shows an entry for "Barracks and Quarters (Special appropriation)" as the heading for the list of civilian employees. Two of the stonemasons became prominent local citizens. James Cornell (1835–1900) was born in England and came to Kinney County in the 1860s, where he established himself as a master builder of well-made stone buildings. He is credited with supervising the building of the officer's quarters and barracks in 1873–74 and the Quartermaster Department Commissary in 1892, along with many of the public buildings constructed in the original town of Brackett in the 1870s. He later grew to be one of the town's most prosperous merchants. His four daughters became the matriarchs of Kinney County's most prominent families. The other was John Taini (1854–1929), an Italian immigrant and skilled stonemason who found employment building the "new post" at Fort Clark. He later moved to Del Rio, where his skills contributed to the building of the Val Verde County courthouse and other public buildings. His construction company returned to Fort Clark in the late 1930s to build both the Service Club and the Officer's Club.

From December 1873 through June 1874, the post return's *Record of Events* reported soldiers were assisting in building the new post. Soldiers felt this was a very distasteful and demeaning work detail, as they labored alongside civilians earning three to seven times a soldier's pay. This practice alone was cause for many desertions.

The "new post" took shape to the west of the antebellum fort, with company officers' quarters sited on an *L*-shaped line facing the emerging barracks row across the spacious parade ground. Six sets of quarters were on the long axis of the *L* and two on the short axis. The Quartermaster

Department plans and specifications called for ten sets of quarters, but only eight were built. The most reasonable explanation is that funding was exhausted. Noteworthy cost-cutting measures included four sets of quarters with only three windows on the side elevation instead of four and Quarters 18–19 being built three feet narrower in width than the other seven sets. Quarters 18–19 is also the only set with no transom above the front door and stonework consisting of rubble-size stones rather than the large blocks evident in the other quarters, suggesting it was the last of the eight sets to be built as funds ran out.

Lieutenant William Paulding's sketch map of Fort Clark in 1874 is the first to show the new officers' quarters. The reports of Acting Assistant Surgeon Donald Jackson and Assistant Surgeon Passmore Middleton, United States Army, in *War Department, Surgeon-General's Office, Circular No. 8*, dated May 1, 1875, are the first official record of the new officers' quarters: "Nine new buildings [includes the Commanding Officer's Quarters; see chapter 4] are now completed for officers' quarters; they are built of stone, two stories high, with porch in front, and back buildings."

An early compliment paid these quarters by army wife occupant Frances Mullen Boyd in her 1895 book *Cavalry Life in Tent and Field* captures the nostalgia felt in 1875, only one year after their completion:

> *Our first home…with double parlors on the ground floor and two large bedrooms above seemed delightful.…Those luxuriant green vines covered our porches so closely as to form perfect little arbors. At least two hammocks were swung on every veranda.…Our limestone houses were toned by the moon's magic influence into poetic beauty, with their shading vines and groups of dainty ladies in white and gallant officers in uniform.*

The Commanding General of the Army, William Tecumseh Sherman, visited Fort Clark for four days in March 1882. His inspection concluded that Fort Clark was the most expensive post in Texas, a waste of money and should be closed. His departure was duly noted in the post return, and remarkably, the only thing that changed was more expansion took place.

It was not uncommon for a bachelor officer to occupy an upstairs bedroom as his quarters when the post was overcrowded. Such was the case in 1883, when Lieutenant Francis Henry French of the 19th Infantry lived upstairs in the quarters of his company commander, Captain Richard Vance. Similarly, newly married Lieutenant Will Paulding of the 10th Infantry moved in with his father-in-law Captain Andrew P. Caraher,

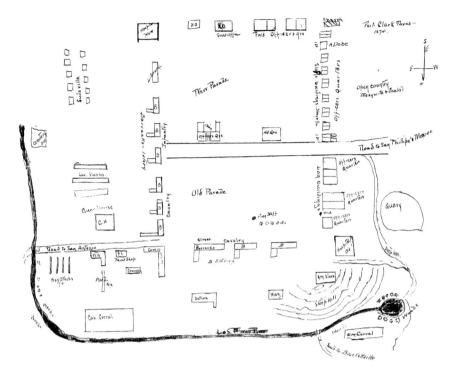

Lieutenant Will Paulding's 1874 map. *Author's collection.*

8th Cavalry, in 1876, when ranked out of his quarters with no other place to go.

This passage from a letter written by Lieutenant French establishes the timeframe when major modifications were made to these eight of Fort Clark's foremost buildings.

> *Fort Clark, Texas*
> *January 31, 1886*
>
> *Genl. Smith is making a great many improvements around the garrison which add materially to the appearance of the post as well as to the comfort of the people. Just now he is straightening and building up the roads around the post, and putting up kitchens at the barracks and raising the officers' kitchens one story.*

This change enclosed the lattice porch between the main area and the kitchen while adding a second story over the kitchen and lattice porch to create additional bedrooms. Only Quarters No. 27–28 has a hip roof on its second-story addition, resulting in limiting headroom. The other seven sets have A-frame roofs. Quarters No. 27–28 is also the only set with second-floor fireplaces. All the others have flues, according to the original plans and specifications. As time passed, many of these quarters had a side porch added and a frame room built onto the back of the kitchen. As with the rest of the post, the luxuries of indoor plumbing and electricity did not come until over a decade or more into the twentieth century. Most of these quarters now have second- or third-generation floors and ceilings.

As with the majority of post buildings, these quarters were built employing pier and beam foundations with distinctive ground-level vents, sometimes referred to as "dog houses," to allow for air flow under the first floor. So soundly built are these foundations that sagging and creaky floors are the exception. Of special note is Quarters No. 11, where later civilian owners unwittingly sealed the vents and the wooden floors quickly rotted, forcing replacement with concrete floors.

Post Surgeon Dr. John Vance Lauderdale wrote in early 1887,

> *We have selected the Quarters next door to the General* [No. 28] *but will not be able to get them for several days. We have stone houses two stories high, deep verandahs in front, also a row of small shade trees round the large parade which must be a mile round. The houses are built for looks as well as durability. We have a nice large house—larger and more convenient than any quarters we have ever found in the Army.*

Assistant Post Surgeon Dr. Edgar Mearns wrote in a letter to his wife dated Sunday, November 6, 1892,

> *We are batching together* [with Dr. William B. Davis] *on Hosp. bunks in his old quarters, the same occupied by Dr. McCreery* [George], *in which he lived several years. I think I will select this house, as it is known as the doctor's house and is vacant, and as good as any other I could get, except one near Col. Lazelle* [Henry Martyn, USMA 1855, commanding the 18th Infantry and the post] *from which I would perhaps be more certain of being ousted by someone with more rank. The house will do about as well as your present house at Snelling* [Fort Snelling, Minnesota]. *Two stories, back yard with high fence, hennery, shed, + outhouse; front yard with vines, grass, flowers; double house. Lieut. Steele* [Charles Lee, USMA 1879, 18th Infantry] *next door.*

The impression these quarters left on an enlisted man, Sergeant Maynard H. McKinnon, in 1917, is also worth sharing:

This little garden spot is caused by several springs which rise here and form Marse [Las Moras] River which flows thru the grounds. You don't know how good it seemed to have green grass and some real trees. The houses are all old southern style and very antique as this is the oldest post in use in the U.S. having been built in 1848 [1852].

Presented below are the complete 1873 Quartermaster Department plans and specifications for these quarters.

PLANS AND SPECIFICATIONS OF COMPANY OFFICERS QUARTERS AT FORT CLARK, TEXAS

Stone Work—The stone to be used in all the foundations to be of suitable quality, the stone will be laid on their broadest bed in good lime Mortar, and well bonded, the thickness and height of the walls to be marked on the plans, foundations to be 2'6" thick, in building the foundations air holes should be left to admit circulation of fresh air underneath the floors, the chimney flues to be built 9" by 18" and smoothly plastered inside, to be topped off as shown on plans, fire places to be constructed in the principle rooms, size of opening 2'6" wide and 2'6" high and about 18" deep at the floor, the flue at the throat should be 6" by 24" that is the

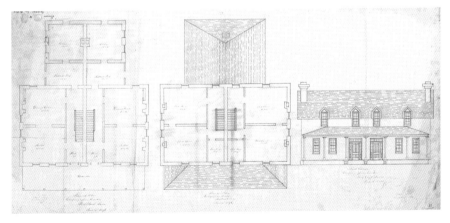

Quartermaster Department plans for Fort Clark's Company Officers Quarters, 1873. *National Archives Record Group 77.*

throat is to be smaller in number of square inches than the Chimney flue, and constructed in the Customary manner. Each flue should be provided with a 7" sheet iron pipe thimble placed about 2 feet below the ceiling. The thickness of the wall to be 18" and the longitudinal partition 12 inches thus allowing the foundation to project 3 inch on the outside, on the inside projection the floor plates are to be laid. On the top of the wall a plate 2'x8" will be laid masoned and anchored to the walls, this plate will give steadiness to the walls and at the same time serve as plate and support to rafters and tie beams.

Mortar—The mortar to be composed of fresh burnt lime and coarse sharp sand in such proportion as will ensure a good and strong cement, the lime to be thoroughly slaked at least one week before its use.

SPECIFICATION OF THE WORKMANSHIP AND BILL OF MATERIAL REQUIRED FOR THE ERECTION AND COMPLETION OF A BUILDING FOR COMPANY OFFICERS QUARTERS AT FORT CLARK, TEXAS ACCORDING TO THE ACCOMPANYING PLANS, SECTIONS, AND ELEVATIONS FOR THE SAME

Dimensions—The building will be 55'6" long by 34 feet wide with an extension in rear of same for kitchen and servants room, said extension to be 25'6" by 17 feet with 10 feet space between floor and ceiling in main building 8'6" in rear building, for dimensions and arrangements of the interior reference is to be made to the plans.

Excavation—The excavation of the foundation is to be 18 inches deep or to the hard ground, after the ground has been leveled and 3 feet wide at the bottom. The foundation to the longitudinal partition is to be the same depth but 2'6" wide at the bottom. The earth from the excavation to be removed to such points as may be directed or spread to an even grade descending from the building.

Carpenter work—All floor and ceiling joists to be laid 16" apart from centers, to be well bridged with 2" by 2" bridging. The wooden partitions to be made of 2" x 6" studding mortised and nailed to double floor joists. Ceiling joists to be well spiked together where they rest on the partition and at the outer ends to be well secured to the wall plates, in the halls staircases will be constructed resting on three stringers made of 2" plank. Stairs to be made in the usual way. In the second story there will be arranged four bedrooms, and bathroom, size and arrangements shown on plan of second story. Dormer windows will lighten the upper halls and chambers in connection with the gable windows. Rafters will be laid 2 feet apart well braced to the tie beams, the collar beams will serve as ceiling joists in the upper halls chambers. Rafters to be sheathed with pine Common boards and covered with shingles laid not over 4½" to the weather. Door and window frames to be made of 2" dressed pine to be well secured and masoned to the walls. Door casings to be plain beaded with a band moulding of a suitable pattern in the outside face, to be five inch well nailed to frame, baseboards to be beaded and not less than 6" wide.

Finally—All material to be of the best quality finish that can be obtained and all work to be done in a workmanlike manner, in accordance with the plans and general intent and meaning of these specifications so as to secure a complete and permanent job in all respects as far as practice.

BILL OF MATERIAL

85	2×10	15'	First floor joists		30	2×8	10'	Front gallery joists
85	2×10	17'	Second floor joists		29	2×4	11'	Front gallery ceiling joists
52	2×10	9'	Hall joists		40	2×6	12'	Front gallery rafters
70	2×8	24'	Rafters		3	2×6	18'	Hip rafters
35	2×8	21'	Collar braces		4,500 ft			Sheathing
68	2×4	6'	Braces for rafters		45,000			Shingles
40	2×8	15'	Kitchen floor joists		6,000 ft	1¼		Yellow pine matched flooring
30	2×8	20'	Kitchen rafters		5,500 ft	⅞		Yellow pine matched ceiling
28	2×6	16'	Kitchen ceiling joists		800 ft			Beaded base boards 8in wide
28	2×4	10'	Kitchen rafter braces		2			Front doorframes Complete
50	2×4	12'	Rafters and studding		4			Outside doorframes 3×76

170	2×6	10'	Studding 1st floor	18				Inside partition doorframes
170	2×6	9'	Studding 2nd floor	8				Dormer windows
260	4×8	LFT	Oak lintels	18				Window frames sash & blinds complete
1000	2×2	LFT	Bridging	304				Perches masonry
20	6×6	11'	Front gallery sills & plates	851				Yards plastering
8	6×6	9'	Front gallery posts					

RECAPITULATION

17,443	Feet framing lumber at $75 per thousand	$1,308.22
4500	Feet sheathing 1 lumber at $75 per thousand	$337.50
45,000	Shingles at $8.50 per thousand	$382.50
6,000	Feet 1¼ yellow pine flooring at $90 per thousand	$540.00
5,500	Feet ⅞ yellow pine ceiling at $80 per thousand	$440.00
8000	Beaded baseboards @ 6 cents per foot	$48.00
51	Door and doorframes, window frames and sash blinds complete including lining @ $18	$918.00
307	Perches masonry at $4.50	$1,381.50
850	Yds plastering at 50 ct	$425.00
2	Staircases per building	$225.00
	Hardware nails	$150.00
	Carpenter labor	$800.00
		$6,955.72
	In today's dollars	$182,538.84

The above estimate is for one building, ten are required.

As a personal footnote to the narrative of these quarters, I had the good

Group of officers and ladies of the 8th Cavalry and 19th Infantry on the porch of Quarters No. 27 in 1884. *Author's collection.*

Officers' Row in the 1920s with Quarters No. 12–13 on the right. *Author's collection.*

Carl Ekmark images from Wednesday, June 8, 1938. *Upper left*: Quarters 12–13; *center*: Quarters 25–26; *upper right*: Quarters 21–22; *lower left*: Quarters 14–15; *lower right*: Quarters 18–19. *Author's collection.*

fortune to own Quarters No. 25 and live there for fifteen rewarding years. Although spacious and solidly built, the quarters were a nightmare to heat and cool. Once the summer heat or the cold of winter penetrated the eighteen-inch-thick rock walls, it became near impossible to reverse. The common flue in the kitchen, where a wood-burning cookstove once stood, always allowed me to smell what my neighbor was cooking. I shall forever miss that big old house, as it had a remarkable character and history that comforted me.

1874

ADJUTANT'S QUARTERS (QUARTERS NO. 20)

Quarters No. 20 today. *Photo by author.*

ADJUTANT'S QUARTERS (QUARTERS #20)
ERECTED DURING THE 1873–1875 EXPANSION OF FORT CLARK TO ACCOMMODATE AND SUPPORT AN ENTIRE REGIMENT, THIS STRUCTURE DIFFERS FROM OTHER QUARTERS ON THE LINE IN THAT IT IS A SINGLE DWELLING RATHER THAN A DUPLEX. THE FIFTH REGIMENT OF THE U.S. CAVALRY WAS GARRISONED HERE FROM 1921 TO 1941 AND DURING THAT TIME THE REGIMENTAL ADJUTANT, WHO PERFORMED ESSENTIAL CLERICAL DUTIES FOR THE REGIMENTAL COMMANDER, LIVED WITHIN THESE WALLS. THE CORE OF THIS BUILDING IS A THREE-ROOM HALL AND PARLOR PLAN COMPOSED OF ADOBE, FEATURING A SYMMETRICAL FRONT AND STONE CHIMNEY AT EACH END. ADDITIONS WERE MADE IN 1904 AND 1944.
—RTHL, 1999

Quarters No. 20 was built by the United States Army in 1874. This single-story structure is constructed of local stone and adobe and situated in the line of company grade officer's quarters. The most unique and significant historic use of this set of quarters was as the designated quarters for the adjutant of the 5th United States Cavalry Regiment from 1921 until 1941. Today, the property continues to fulfill its original intended purpose of providing family housing.

In the early 1870s, Fort Clark rapidly expanded to accommodate and support the regimental-size garrison needed to deal effectively with the increasing number of Indian depredations along the border. The post doubled in size from 1873 to 1875. The Quartermaster "Plans and Specifications of Company Officers Quarters at Fort Clark, Texas," dated 1873, includes the statement, "The above estimate is for one building, ten are required." The ground was laid out for ten buildings; however, only eight were built. This observation is critical to the location, plan and construction materials of Quarters No. 20.

Space on the long side of the L was allowed for eight sets of quarters. The angle point of the L was left vacant and was not filled with a building until fifteen years later, in 1888, when a double set of staff officers' quarters was completed (see chapter 10). Between Quarters 18–19 and 21–22, there was also a vacant space. In that space, Quarters No. 20 first appears on the map of Fort Clark in the "Outline Description of the Military Posts in the Division of the Missouri," dated April 15, 1876. This reference also states, "Officers' quarters, twenty sets built of stone and one built of adobe." By process of elimination, the adobe set is Quarters No. 20. This conclusion is further substantiated by a description of the post in 1874 found in the memoirs of Lieutenant William Paulding, 10th Infantry: "South of this is an open piece of ground and the new post is built there. The houses are all two story double houses, except one, which is adobe and is single set." Lieutenant Paulding's hand-sketched map confirms Quarters No. 20 as the adobe set.

To fill the vacant space between Quarters 18–19 and 21–22, a simple set of quarters (No. 20) was constructed of adobe, a readily available and inexpensive local material. The original floor plan was also simple: a single story with just three rooms and a fireplace on each end. This plan so closely mirrors the plan from the sets of Fort Clark's existing log officers' quarters constructed in 1854 that it may have been copied.

Occupancy of Quarters No. 20 in the nineteenth century was characterized by the distasteful practice—at least to officers' wives—of "turning out"

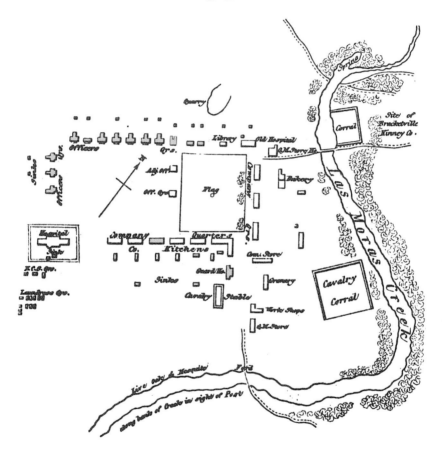

Plan of Fort Clark, 1876. Buildings in gray are now Recorded Texas Historic Landmarks. *From* Outline Description of the Military Posts in the Division of the Missouri.

another officer to secure quarters. A senior officer, even by brevet rank, could force an officer junior to himself to relinquish a set of quarters simply on demand. The junior moved out, the senior moved in and the junior then looked for someone he outranked so he could continue the process. The officers' ladies referred to the ordeal as "falling bricks," as it could, at times, cause wholesale moves, affecting an entire garrison.

After decades of grievances from army wives and the advent of long-term, often permanent, stationing of units at the same post following the First World War, the practice of turning out faded away. In its place developed the custom of designating or reserving a set of quarters for the officer assigned to a particular duty position. Traditionally, the only designated quarters on a post was the house built for the commanding officer, always the largest and most dominant. Some posts also reserved quarters for staff officers (field grade officers in the rank of major or lieutenant colonel). At Fort Clark, Quarters 25–26 and 27–28 constituted "Staff Row," and later, Quarters 23–24 was built to specifically serve as staff officer quarters. The policy became standard and is still in use in the army today.

In the fall of 1921, the 5th United States Cavalry Regiment conducted a permanent change of station from Camp Marfa to Fort Clark. In the quiet time between World Wars I and II, the 5th Cavalry became indelibly associated with Fort Clark, garrisoning the post for a generation, until 1941. During the 5th Cavalry era, several sets of quarters were designated to be occupied by officers assigned specific duty positions. Quarters No. 24 was designated for the colonel of the regiment and No. 20, only three doors away, for the regimental adjutant.

The position of regimental adjutant was an unattractive one normally filled by a senior lieutenant or a junior captain. The adjutant, for all practical purposes, was a glorified clerk for the regimental commander. However, the adjutant did perform the essential function of managing the endless flow of regimental paperwork and keeping the colonel out of trouble in that department. It was and still is a thankless job, involving long hours of tedious attention to detail. Quarters No. 20 was, then, a fairly obvious choice for the adjutant's house. It was in proximity to the colonel's house and otherwise had no other status or desirability due to its size and style. In 1994, one David R. Hollingsworth and his sister, Virginia H. Cunningham, visited Fort Clark to participate in the fort's Elderhostel Program. It was a homecoming, since their father was an officer in the 5th Cavalry and David and Virginia spent their childhood, in the 1930s, at Fort Clark. When their father was the regimental adjutant, they lived in No. 20. When he was promoted to captain and reassigned to command a troop, they moved into Quarters No. 19.

Maps of the post and comparative analysis of period photographs reflect a change to the appearance of Quarters No. 20 at the beginning of the twentieth century. A post map, dated April 12, 1904, shows a wing now

View of Quarters No. 20 (*center*) from the 1920s. The concrete sidewalk dates from 1918. *Author's collection.*

Carl Ekmark image, Wednesday, June 8, 1938. *Author's collection.*

Carl Ekmark image, Wednesday, June 8, 1938. *Author's collection.*

extended to the rear off the south end of the original structure. This frame addition was treated with shiplap siding and later partially stuccoed. Interior walls were plastered. Another small addition was also made to the rear off the north end of the building at this time. Again, wood frame with shiplap siding and interior plaster was the technique of construction. A third addition of another wing was made to the north end sometime after August 1944. It is all frame with clapboard siding.

In the *Report of Inspection of Buildings and Utilities at Fort Clark, Texas,* conducted from October 17 to 20, 1928, and published by the Office of the Quartermaster, Headquarters 8th Corps Area, Fort Sam Houston, Texas, a detailed description of Quarters No. 20 was made, as follows:

Building Number 20

Married Officers' Quarters—single set
       Construction—one story stone and adobe
       Foundation—stone
       Roof—wood shingles
       Floors—wood
       Dimensions—30' x 43' 6" (main building
                       30' x 15' (wing

[Also stated are the inspecting officer's recommendations for repair to the building.]

Renew roofs of front porch and additions with wood shingles.
Apply two coats of paint to exterior woodwork.
Provide three sets of one tread steps, concrete.
Treads to be 24" x 4'.
Replace 50' of window screening.
Replace front porch floor with concrete.
Repoint exterior stone work.
Interior of No. 20
Not inspected. (Hqs, 8th Corps Area, 56)

Quarters No. 20 has maintained its architectural integrity while standing the test of time since 1874. Footsteps echo from the countless army families who made it their home. Throughout its existence, the tiny adobe structure has retained its individuality and unique character, nestled in among its larger, more imposing two-story stone neighbors.

1874

GUARDHOUSE

Old Guard House Museum today. *Photo by author.*

Killis P. Almond Jr.'s 1981 Preservation Plan notes:

This is a one-story rectangular plan building with a hipped roof. The front (north) porch is a concrete deck with a cement parged stone perimeter wall foundation. Wood columns divide the porch into ten bays with a single line two-by-four wood railing with intermediate four-by-four posts. Window and door openings have timber lintels and sills. Windows are typically six-over-one wood double hung sash. Stonework is random coursed ashlar which is quarry-faced. This building was constructed as the guard house during the nineteenth century and still retains several of the iron barred cells. An historic shed extension to the rear (south) remains but is in poor condition. There has been moderate to extensive mortar pointing and cement parging. Lower one-light sash reveals mortises which originally held six-light muntins in place. The original porch was shed and did not span the full length of the building. The wood columns have been undercut and raised upon concrete plinths.

The Guardhouse was built by the United States Army in 1874 of local limestone at a cost of $5,670.65 and is a contributing structure to the National Register Historic District of Fort Clark. The building is Fort Clark's second guard house. On many frontier posts, the guard house is the only remaining building, as they were typically built of stone. Guard houses served two purposes: to house the soldiers on guard duty and as a confinement facility for soldiers accused of both minor and serious infractions of military order and discipline. Today, the building serves as the Old Guardhouse Museum and houses the collections of the Fort Clark Historical Society.

Of Fort Clark's first guard house, located on the site of today's Service Club, Inspector General Colonel Joseph K.F. Mansfield noted in 1856,

> [The] *Guard House is of stone with a good prison attached with 3 cells for solitary confinement, 1 general cell & 1 prison room—a guard of 9 men. There were 12 prisoners, 4 deserters, 7 drunkenness & one under sentence for stabbing another; as the last case was a severe one I recommended him to the favour of the Commanding Officer of the department.*

Always in continuous occupation and operation, the guard house was the only post building that never closed. The necessity of a guard house grew out of the obvious need for security; it was also a means for the enforcement of military order and discipline. A 1997 study of the U.S. Quartermaster General standardized plans, 1866–1942, by the Corps of Engineers, summarizes the evolution and common architectural features of the post guard house:

The guard house evolved as a separate building type, notably at frontier posts, after the Army stopped the construction of walled or fortified installations during the mid-nineteenth century. Without surrounding fortifications, the free-standing guard house evolved to serve as the central point to guard the post and hold prisoners. At frontier forts, where the isolated post could be approached from many directions, the guard house was located apart from the main parade ground, often behind the barracks. The typical guard house constructed during the late nineteenth century was a one-story, square or rectangular building with a hipped roof and a full-facade veranda.

Although Quartermaster General Montgomery Meigs issued a standard plan for guard houses in 1872, no examples are known to exist. Guard house design was typically left to local commanders, who generally followed a proven model of sturdy stone construction and a floor plan that included an office for the officer of the guard, a guard room to house off-duty soldiers of the guard detail, a large prison room to hold general prisoners and individual cells for more serious offenders. Fort Clark's guard house closely mirrors this model, with the addition of a latrine in the twentieth century. Perhaps unique to Fort Clark's guard house, there is only one cell without a window, which is believed to have been used for solitary confinement, and one-of-a-kind heavy cell doors fabricated from the iron tires of wagon wheels.

Prisoners knew the post guard house to be a harsh and pitiless place to be imprisoned. Despite a change of guards every twenty-four hours, there were surprisingly few recorded escapes, perhaps owing to the lack of time for guard complacency to set in. A prisoner also knew that if he attempted escape, a sentinel "will fire upon him." Even so, on Thursday, January 13, 1887, the officer of the guard at Fort Clark, Texas, Lieutenant Francis H. French, 19th Infantry, recorded in his diary,

Shortly after tattoo the special patrol galloped up to the guard house and stated that a prisoner out with the night cart had escaped. The corporal in charge of the party came in with the other prisoner and verified the report. Think it was a piece of great carelessness in the corporal to let the man escape and believe he ought to be court martialed.... This is the first time a prisoner has escaped from a guard under my control.

Historically, the guard house was the responsibility of the officer of the guard. This essential duty rotated among the junior officers (lieutenants) of the garrison and lasted twenty-four hours. Guard mount took place each morning in the vicinity of the guard house or, frequently, on the main parade ground, depending on the whim of the post commander. It was not uncommon for guard mount to be an elaborate affair, with the regimental band playing and the entire garrison witnessing the event. At guard mount, the soldiers coming on guard duty were inspected by the new officer of the guard and broken down into three "reliefs" based on the number of soldiers needed to man various guard posts or sentry boxes, walking posts and mounted posts around the fort or to guard prisoners out on work detail. Soldiers spent the twenty-four-hour period in increments of two hours as sentinels standing a guard post, followed by four hours off. A soldier was forbidden by army regulations from removing his uniform or accoutrements while on guard duty. "Off" time was spent in the guard room, passing time by engaging in the time-honored soldiers' pursuits of sleeping, playing card games, telling tall tales and gossiping. The guard room also served as the garrison courtroom where courts-martial were held.

Throughout the twenty-four-hour period the officer of the guard got very little rest as he was required to inspect the guard at specific times and oversee the prisoners. Subordinate to the officer of the guard was the sergeant of the guard (a senior noncommissioned officer) and the corporals of the guard or commanders of the relief. These individuals worked and slept in what is now the Swanson Archives room. The officer of the guard's office also had interior access to the cell block. The daily routine of the garrison was vested in the officer of the guard. It was his responsibility to ensure that all "calls" were sounded at the appointed time by the musician of the guard, that the guard flag detail hoisted the proper flag briskly at the first note of reveille, as the morning gun was simultaneously fired by another detail of the guard, and that the flag was lowered with the firing of the evening gun at the last note of retreat. He recorded all his actions and any incidents during his tour of duty in the guard book.

Here are several more extracts from the diary of Lieutenant Francis H. French, 19th Infantry, when he was officer of the guard at Fort Clark in the late nineteenth century:

> **Sunday, May 6, 1883**—*Sgt. Kibbets* [Seminole Scout] *reported Blanco absent from stables this morning. Felt badly to punish him the first in the Detachment, but was compelled to do so. Had him confined in the Guard House and shall prefer charges against him.*
>
> **Saturday, March 8, 1884**—*While inspecting prisoner's room before marching off, one named Lang Troop "E" said "I will if I like"*

when I told him to put "Sir" on his answers to me. Think the fellow is crazy. Had him locked up in a cell, and after marching off preferred charges against him.

Wednesday, January 6, 1886—*Marched on guard and spent the day quietly at the guard house, my stomach bothering me more than before. Only left the guard house to inspect sentinels and for lunch and dinner. Capt. Hall came down to see me a few minutes and the General called to give an order about the paymaster's safe. Officer of the Day caught me sleeping just before tattoo, but said it was all right on account of my trouble. He inspected just after midnight.*

Friday, April 23, 1886—*…Slept until after three o'clock when Officer of the Day inspected. After tattoo a wagon drove up bringing from Del Rio under guard a member of the orchestra of the troupe that performed here a short time ago as a deserter from the Band of the 16th Infantry.*

The new century brought another generation of soldiers to Fort Clark to train for the Great War. They quickly experienced this most unloved of any post building firsthand, ingraining the opinion that the guard house was the most detested building on Fort Clark. The letters of Sergeant Maynard H. McKinnon, Ambulance Company No. 7, bring to light the timeless reality of a soldier doing his duty at the Fort Clark guard house.

Sept. 8, 1917—*Whenever a prisoner goes to wash or to his outfit to eat a guard follows behind, and a guard just brought two back from dinner and yelled as they came in, "Corporal of the guard—two prisoners" and as I was turnkey at the time I locked them up in their cells. When you're a prisoner you have to do all such nasty work as cleaning out the toilets, gathering up garbage and clean[ing] out stables for the mule companies.*

Sept. 28, 1917—*We have the same bunch in here yet with about seven more added for drunk & five picked up in a joint last Monday. So the "coop's" about full. I sure will have to get a sheriff's job in order to use my jailer's knowledge.*

Oct. 20, 1917—*I'm at the most cheerless place hereabouts for I'm down to the guard house again. An old tumble down rat covered place, high ceilinged and musty and covered with cobwebs.*

January 7, 1918—*But the old place has a history and I wish I knew it for it must be very interesting. We have a full house now, the most prisoners we ever had, twenty-four in all. They have been coming fast lately, most of them for drunkenness and absence without leave for several over*

Buffalo soldiers of the 10th Cavalry, fresh from their charge up San Juan Hill, congregate on the guard house porch during their four hours off from being sentinels. Note the soldiers lying on bunks, which have been moved from the hot, stuffy guard room to the relative coolness of the porch. *Author's collection.*

The Guard House was always a popular subject for the camera and the shared memory of every soldier who served at Fort Clark. *Author's collection.*

The Old Guard House Museum's first curator, Donald A. Swanson, inspects the cell block, circa 1980s. *Author's collection.*

stayed their Xmas furloughs and my sympathies are strongly for the latter. Some girl from downtown, one from our "red-light" district came to see a prisoner and I had to tell her "nothing doing" for we are not allowed to let them have visitors, especially not of her sort. She was of the dark Spanish type & flashy dressed, low waist, short skirts, high heels and highly painted and I imagine thru her, he landed in the guard house. Anyway, she did not see him that day.

The Old Guardhouse Museum began during the Brown Foundation's Guest Ranch era, 1950–71, as a storage building for a collection of World War II aircraft nose art gathered by Minot Tully Pratt Jr. from the thousands of surplus planes purchased from the U.S. government by Brown and Root for salvage after the war. In 1962, the building was the first to be designated a "Recorded Texas Historic Landmark" by the Texas Historical Commission. The Fort Clark Community Council restored the building in 1976. When the Fort Clark Historical Society was chartered in December 1979—the same month the Fort Clark Historic District was listed in the National Register of Historic Places—the old guard house seemed the appropriate place to display the growing number of Fort Clark artifacts being donated to the society by veterans, visitors and local residents. It was retired U.S. Navy lieutenant commander Donald A. Swanson who, as curator from 1986 to 1996, took the museum to the next level of care by meticulously cataloging the collection and markedly improving the museum's displays. His singular effort in establishing the museum's archives created an invaluable resource for genealogists, researchers and military history buffs. The majority of the current exhibits were designed and created by myself during my curatorship of the museum from 2008 to 2011.

1886 KITCHEN/MESS HALL

1886 Kitchen/Mess Hall today. *Photo by author.*

1886 KITCHEN/MESS HALL

THE EARLIEST MESS ARRANGEMENTS FOR SOLDIERS AT FORT CLARK WERE AROUND OPEN FIRES ALONG LAS MORAS CREEK NEAR THE SPRING. THIS BUILDING IS ONE OF FORT CLARK'S EIGHT REMAINING KITCHENS AND MESS HALLS OUT OF NINE BUILT IN 1886 TO SERVE EACH COMPANY OF ENLISTED MEN. IT IS BUILT WITH LOCALLY QUARRIED LIMESTONE AND FEATURES A PIER AND BEAM FOUNDATION, DOUBLE HUNG WINDOWS, MASONRY OPENINGS SPANNED WITH TIMBER LINTELS, AND TWO CHIMNEYS FOR COOKING AND HEATING. THE BUILDING WAS LATER USED FOR VARIED ADMINISTRATIVE PURPOSES, INCLUDING DAY ROOMS, UNIT OFFICES, AND SUPPLY AND ARMS STORAGE.

—RTHL, 2015

As one of Fort Clark's eight remaining 1886 Kitchen/Mess Halls, this building served varied purposes for the enlisted men of the fort's garrison over six decades, from 1886 to 1944. The building is recognized in the National Register narrative as a contributing structure to the Fort Clark Historic District. This sturdy, unadorned, utilitarian building was experienced by generations of soldiers, from the Indian Wars of the nineteenth century to World War II in the twentieth century. The presence of this building is conclusively linked to Fort Clark's significant contribution to United States Army heritage and architecture.

The earliest mess arrangements for soldiers at Fort Clark were around open fires along Las Moras Creek near the spring. Prior to the late 1870s, the position of cook as a permanent military occupation in the army did not exist, and soldiers alternated trying their best at the culinary art.

> *The soldiers took turns cooking, so most meals were boiled and bad; stew, hash, baked beans, hardtack (often moldy), salt pork (sometimes maggoty), dried apples and potatoes, and coffee. At forts lacking gardens, the men came down with scurvy. Despite the efforts of post surgeons, sanitation was terrible, and disease took a far higher toll than battles with the Indians.*

Many of Fort Clark's early kitchen/mess hall buildings used the practical construction technique of vertical posts (jacal), which was a typical frontier military expedient in Texas.

In 1872, a panel of officers at the War Department, chaired by Army Inspector General Randolph B. Marcy, recommended to the Commanding General of the Army, William T. Sherman, that model plans be adopted for the construction of military buildings. Sherman did not support the recommendation; neither did the Quartermaster General of the Army, Montgomery C. Meigs. However, somehow, the Marcy Board prevailed, and Meigs produced model plans for six building types: company quarters, company officer's quarters, commanding officer's quarters, guard houses, bake houses and hospitals.

The only building in the Fort Clark Historic District built to those model plans is the commanding officers quarters. The model plan for company quarters called for a kitchen and mess room on the first floor, and a variation of this plan may have been used at Fort Clark for the nine kitchen/mess rooms constructed in 1886.

After over a decade and a half of use, the palisado kitchen/mess rooms began to prove inadequate as the post grew to support a regimental-size

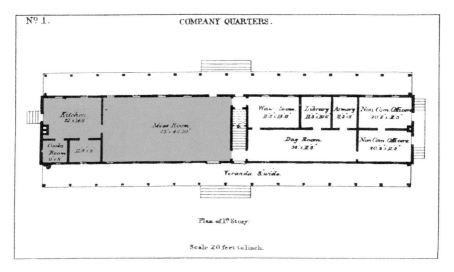

Quartermaster Department Model Plan No. 1 for Company Quarters, 1872. *National Archives Record Group 77.*

garrison—which, by 1886, had swelled to nearly 750 officers and men. At that time, the post commander, Colonel (Brevet Major General) Charles H. Smith, 19th Infantry, embarked on a significant building project such as the post had not experienced for well over a decade. His plan was to build nine stone company kitchens, all on the same plan, with one to be erected immediately behind each infantry barracks and two placed behind each cavalry barracks.

> *Fort Clark, Texas*
> *January 31, 1886*
>
> *Genl. Smith is making a great many improvements around the garrison which add materially to the appearance of the post as well as to the comfort of the people. Just now he is straightening and building up the roads around the post, and putting up kitchens at the barracks and raising the officers' kitchens one story.*

This passage from a letter written by Lieutenant Francis Henry French of the 19th Infantry establishes the construction year of the eight mess halls, which are now some of the historic district's most long-lasting buildings.

Post returns during the construction period account for the employment of only one civilian mason and three civilian carpenters, raising the possibility that the kitchen/mess halls were built using soldier labor under the supervision of skilled civilian craftsmen or an outside contractor. Each kitchen/mess hall was built using native limestone from the fort's own quarry. This stone proved to be of inferior quality, which, over time, has contributed to rising damp issues for many of these buildings. Dimensions are a uniform twenty-seven by sixty-seven feet, with pier and beam foundations and A-frame gabled roofs. Windows are typically six-over-six wood double-hung windows. All masonry openings are spanned with timber lintels. A brick flue chimney is located inside the kitchen end of the building, which allowed for use of an army wood-burning cast-iron range. A second flue chimney at the south end permitted the use of a heating stove in the mess room during the winter months. When viewed from the kitchen end (north elevation, in the case of this building), there is one door on the left side and one centered window. The east elevation has six evenly placed windows, which align with the windows and doors of the west elevation. The rear portion of the east elevation has one closely placed window and, finally, a door; these also align with a window and a door on the west elevation. Ashlar stone was used on the north and east corners.

The placement of door openings points to the likelihood of interior rooms being part of the original floor plan. Again, providing interior rooms for the cooks and noncommissioned officers of the unit would follow the intent of the 1872 model plan. This observation is also supported by the description of the building in 1901: "stone kitchen, shingled roof detached, 6 rooms & kitchen 66'x27'6"."

Of the original nine stone mess halls constructed by the army in 1886, eight remain. One building, the former mess hall for Headquarters Troop 1st Cavalry Brigade, currently serves as the boardroom for Fort Clark Springs Association. Next are the four wings behind Patton Hall and Bullis Hall, all now comfortable homes. Of the four mess halls built behind barracks row, three are still in use—not as kitchens but as residences. The ninth building burned in the 1980s and has been reduced to rubble. All these buildings once served as kitchen/mess halls, and several, including this building, were later used as administrative buildings housing day rooms, unit offices and supply and arms rooms. As a mess hall, the building contained a kitchen at the north end with one or more large army cookstoves and a mess room furnished with long tables and Model 1883 oak mess hall stools, where the soldiers sat and ate their meals family style.

The only specific reference to and detailed description of this building (post building No. 115) is found on page 127 of the *Report of Inspection of*

Buildings and Utilities at Fort Clark, Texas, conducted by Colonel James R. Pourie, Quartermaster Corps, 8th Corps Area Utilities Officer from October 17 to 20, 1928, and published by the Office of the Quartermaster, Headquarters 8th Corps Area, Fort Sam Houston, Texas:

Building Number 115

Mess Hall and Kitchen: Same size and type of construction as No. 107. [One story stone building. Foundation rock. Roof, wood shingles. Floors, wood. Dimensions 27' x 67'.] *Now used as day room.*
  Repoint stone wall, over an area of approximately 18 sq. ft.
  Replace 8 ten by twelve window panes.
  Replace 100 sq. ft. of window screening.
  Rebuild two chimneys.
  Replace six window frames

Interior of No. 115
  Reset two door frames.
  Replaster interior walls, six sq. yards
  Apply one coat of calcimine to interior walls.

This same 1928 inspection report strongly recommended the demolition of the two-story barracks, built in 1874, which this kitchen/mess hall supported. As a result, in 1931, a new two-story barracks was built on the footprint of the 1874 barracks building. At that time, it was also determined to connect the two buildings by filling the twenty-four-foot space between the barracks and the 1886 kitchen/mess hall with a modern troop latrine.

This historic connecting structure, now part of the property, is built with load-bearing walls of webwall limestone veneer with clad frame and clay tile construction. Windowsills are cast stone, lintels are steel and the floor is concrete. This modern latrine replaced an outdoor privy in use for decades. Finally, the troopers of Troop "A," 5th U.S. Cavalry, could benefit from indoor plumbing with hot showers, sinks and flush toilets after a hard day of soldiering.

Since 1886, the building has experienced interior alterations and remodeling to suit either the needs of the army or, now, the requirements of the private civilian owner. This building has experienced the least exterior modifications of any of the eight remaining 1886 kitchen/mess halls, with just one door opening becoming a window. All other masonry openings

One of Fort Clark's 1886 Kitchen/Mess Halls in the 1920s. *Author's collection.*

Interior of the 1886 Kitchen/Mess Hall used by Troop A, 5th Cavalry in the 1930s. *Author's collection.*

Troopers of the 112th Cavalry eat a hardy meal on the eve of World War II. *Author's collection.*

In 1959, the cast and crew of John Wayne's film *The Alamo* chow down in the 1886 kitchen/mess hall, which is now the Fort Clark Springs Association boardroom. *Author's collection.*

remain unchanged. This building ranks as the best surviving example of the original 1886 kitchen/mess halls in the Historic District and perhaps the only one of its type in Texas.

This kitchen/mess hall served the garrison nearly sixty years until Fort Clark closed on August 28, 1944. This 1886 kitchen/mess hall is a classic and admirable model of utilitarian U.S. Army architecture from the Indian Wars of the late nineteenth century, with a design suited to the needs of the expanding post garrison in the mid-1880s. The building continues to provide shelter and comfort as originally intended and is being responsibly maintained in a good state of repair by the current owner. Of the eight remaining single-story stone kitchen/mess halls in the Fort Clark Historic District, all but this example have experienced irreversible unsympathetic modifications. Only this kitchen/mess hall stands out as essentially unaltered and an exemplary model of preservation.

This 1886 kitchen/mess hall is an exceptional example of nineteenth-century utilitarian army architecture remaining intact in the Fort Clark Historic District. This building and its siblings may well be the vestige of only a handful of Indian Wars–period single-story stone kitchen/mess halls left on any army post in the nation and perhaps the sole original examples of this type of military construction still standing in Texas.

1888

STAFF OFFICERS' QUARTERS (PATTON HOUSE)

Staff Officers' Quarters, the Patton House, today. *Photo by author.*

Staff Officers Quarters No. 23–24 was built by the United States Army
in 1888, as evidenced by the incised cornerstones of the building. This
building is constructed of local limestone and situated at the end of the line
of company grade officer's quarters. A definitive showpiece throughout its

existence, the property continues to fulfill its original intended purpose as family housing.

Killis P. Almond Jr.'s 1981 Preservation Plan notes:

This two-story stone building has a "T" plan with hipped roofs. This house follows closely the plan of the typical officer's quarters but departs from the norm by having a full height second floor and hipped roofs of relatively shallow pitch. The stonework is also more refined, being regularly coursed, squared ashlar which had been pitchfaced. The porch at the front (east) is also a double gallery with chamfered solid wood columns. Windows are typically six-over-six, double hung wood sash with tooled stone lintels and stone sills. The building is in excellent condition. The roof is covered with asphalt composition shingles and porches have been added and enclosed at the rear of the building.

Of the building's origins, Post Surgeon John V. Lauderdale wrote in his diary on Tuesday, January 17, 1888, "I see that they have drawn stone and broken ground for a new set of quarters to be built just at the angle looking towards the target range. It will be a set of double quarters about like the others in the same line."

The good doctor would be proven wrong in thinking these quarters would be "about like the others." Far from it: this double set of quarters was not only unique but also spacious and elegant by army standards. Each set had double parlors, separated by a distinctive arch, containing large oak pocket doors and a sizeable dining room, pantry and kitchen. Upstairs were four bedrooms and a full-length balcony across the front of the second story. It was also the only quarters with a tin roof. The quarters were decidedly Victorian, with tasteful decorative features—such as massive banisters not found elsewhere on the post, even in the quarters of the commanding officer. This was, no doubt, a highly desirable set of quarters for majors or lieutenant colonels. During the late 1880s, when these quarters were built, the Quartermaster Department made a concerted effort to construct buildings of greater architectural stature that projected an increased awareness of the prestige of the military. Army architects designed larger, more elegant officer housing in contemporary, nationally popular architectural styles; Colonial Revival architecture dominated the army construction of this era. Frame additions to the rear of these quarters can be seen in the panoramic photographs of the late 1930s. Where Quarters No. 23 has a simple flagstone patio on the side elevation, Quarters No. 24 has large first- and second-floor screened porches.

The second-floor front porch was remembered by Maria Brace Kimball, wife of Post Surgeon Major James P. Kimball, in her book, *A Soldier-Doctor of Our Army*:

> *The days in September were very hot, but the starry nights on our balcony were delightfully cool after nine o'clock when the "Gulf breeze" arrives. Promptly as Tattoo is sounding the cool current from the ocean rushes in across a hundred miles of scorching prairie. Blinds creak, doors slam, windows rattle, the horizon is aglow with heat lightning, the earth seems astir and alive again. The garrison wakes up, neighbors talk from house to house and even exchange visits. A blessed gift this sea wind to the nights of Texas!*

In the fall of 1921, the 5th U.S. Cavalry Regiment conducted a permanent change of station from Camp Marfa to Fort Clark. In the quiet time between World Wars I and II, the 5th Cavalry became indelibly associated with Fort Clark, garrisoning the post for a generation, until 1941. The activation of the 1st Cavalry Brigade Headquarters in early 1923 forced the 5th Cavalry commander (then Colonel William Dennison Forsyth) to relinquish the Commanding Officer's House to the brigade commander (a general officer) and move (an event remembered by the colonel's daughter,

Staff Officers' Quarters Nos. 23–24 at the beginning of the twentieth century. *Author's collection.*

Elizabeth Forsyth Scheuber, then seven years old) into the second-best set of quarters on the post, Quarters No. 24 (second best based on size, quality of construction and being protected from the weather by Quarters No. 23). From that point until the regiment departed, Quarters No. 24 was designated for the colonel of the 5th Cavalry Regiment. The most prominent occupant was Colonel George S. Patton Jr., from July to December 1938.

These quarters are named for Patton, the highest-ranking officer to ever occupy them. Patton graduated from West Point in the class of 1911 and, in the summer of 1938, was assigned to command the 5th Cavalry Regiment at Fort Clark. Patton arrived at Fort Clark on July 24, 1938, and sent a note to his wife, Beatrice, of his initial impressions of his new duty station,

> *San Antonio is very quaint and I think you will like it....*[Fort] *Clark is 138 miles due west....I think we will like it. Gen J.* [Kenyon A. Joyce, commanding the 1st Cavalry Brigade] *runs the post and I run the regiment, which makes it very nice. The Joyces were delighted to see me and are more human than* [they were] *at* [Fort] *Myer....All one can do here is to Ride-Read-Write & Swim.*

Patton quickly set about preparing his quarters for his family's arrival and again wrote Beatrice of his preparations,

> *The house is beginning to look swell. I had a new room built for a butler's pantry and bought a sink for it. I also am having the garden fenced with a 6-foot lattice fence, which should be finished by the end of September. All work here has to be done by soldiers. So as not to make them hate me I have them do the work on their own time and pay them for it.*

Patton enjoyed Fort Clark and its outdoor life, which restored him to health. His daughter, Ruth Ellen, in her book *The Button Box*, reflected that the family all loved Fort Clark and her mother loved it as much as any post she had ever lived on. Patton's hopes of remaining in Texas came to an abrupt end when on December 1, 1938, after only four short months at Fort Clark, the War Department reassigned him to replace Jonathan M. Wainwright (who was promoted to brigadier general and assigned to Fort Clark) as commander of the 3rd Cavalry in Washington, D.C.

In the *Report of Inspection of Buildings and Utilities at Fort Clark, Texas*, conducted from October 17 to 20, 1928, and published by the Office of the

Quartermaster, Headquarters 8th Corps Area, Fort Sam Houston, Texas, a detailed description of Quarters No. 23 and 24 was made, as follows:

Building Number 23 and 24
Married Officers' Quarters—double set.

Construction—two story stone
Foundation—rock
Roof—in, with box gutter
Floors—wood
Dimensions—56' x 34' (main building)
—46' x 34' 6" (wings in rear)
A two story screened in porch extends along the front of the building.
Paint exterior woodwork two coats in conformity with post color scheme.
Provide framed screens for six foundation vents.
Replace five downspouts.
Replace few wood shingles over back porch.
Replace two sets of four tread concrete steps at north side entrance. Treads to be 12" x 4'.
Replace one set of four tread steps, concrete, at rear entrance. Treads to be 12" x 7'.
Front porch floor is in good condition.
Replace 150 ft. of window screening.
Repair two 2'8" x 6'8" screen doors.
Repair flashing around chimneys.

Interior of No. 23
Replace 30 brick in fireplaces of living and dining rooms.
Replace 220 ft. of flooring in kitchen.
Clean, sand and refinish floors of main building.
Paint interior wall one coat.
Paint interior woodwork one coat.
Repair approximately 40 ft. of plaster throughout.

Interior of No. 24
Interior of this set of quarters is being completely refinished and no repairs are recommended at this time.
Note: A careful examination of the tin roof developed the fact that it should be replaced with asbestos shingles and the box gutter replaced with an overhanging roof.

Staff Officers' Quarters No. 23–24 on Wednesday, June 8, 1938. *Author's collection.*

The last soldiers, Captain Stanley J. Sawicki and Chief Warrant Officer Jimmie E. Ray, turned out the lights and departed Fort Clark on August 28, 1944. For the next two years, the venerable post had a small contingent of civilian caretakers from the Corps of Engineers. On October 29, 1946, the War Assets Administration sold Fort Clark to the highest bidder, the Texas Railway Equipment Company (a subsidiary of Brown and Root), for $411,250. The new owners sold the lumber and fixtures from the World War II temporary construction and quickly recovered the purchase price of the fort. Almost 1,500 buildings were demolished for salvage. Olla Belle Dahlstrom, wife of Frederick L. "Slim" Dahlstrom, owner of the Texas Railway Equipment Company, is said to have been the driving force behind saving over eighty historic buildings from the wrecking ball. Herman Brown, of Brown and Root, particularly loved Fort Clark and, in the early 1950s, opened the Fort Clark Guest Ranch to share his treasure. Herman chose the Patton House for his vacation retreat, where he entertained an impressive assortment of powerful Texans, including Governor John Connally, Senator Lloyd Bentsen and President Lyndon Baines Johnson, on hunting trips and for the inevitable political "powwows." Following a stay at the Patton House in October 1955, Lady Bird Johnson sent a thank-you letter to Margarett Root Brown:

President Lyndon Baines Johnson on the Patton House porch swing (made from an old army bunk) in the 1960s, with George Brown on his left. *Chris A. Hale collection.*

Our weekend with you at Fort Clark was a sort of debut for Lyndon and me and I couldn't have dreamed up one under happier circumstances or with people we would have loved as much to sit around and talk with....Many, many thanks for giving us such a happy time in a setting we have always loved and with people whose friendship we cherish. [LBJ Library. At the time, LBJ was the Senate majority leader.]

The Patton House is meticulously preserved and maintained by the Hale family as a stately jewel in the crown of the historic district, never failing to impress with its unspoken dignity.

PART II

THE TWENTIETH CENTURY

1932

POST THEATER

The Fort Clark Post Theater today, painted in the 1928 post color scheme of light gray, ivory cream and seal brown. *Photo by author.*

POST THEATER

CONSTRUCTED IN 1932, THIS BUILDING REPLACED AN EARLIER FORT CLARK POST HALL THAT SERVED AS A CHURCH, COURTROOM, THEATER, AND RECREATIONAL CENTER. A UTILITARIAN MILITARY DESIGN OF CLEAR SPAN CONSTRUCTION, BRICK WALLS, AND A STUCCO VENEER, THE BUILDING ALSO EXHIBITS CLASSICAL STYLE INFLUENCES IN ITS PILASTERS, ARCHED WINDOWS, AND PEDIMENT. A POPULAR MOVIE THEATER UNTIL THE FORT WAS CLOSED IN 1944, IT LATER BECAME A TOWN HALL FOR THE FORT CLARK SPRINGS COMMUNITY.

—RTHL, 1997

This inscription is the least accurate and the most historically misleading of any RTHL marker in the district. As this updated narrative will establish, there is little or no connection between the Post Theater and the post hall of the nineteenth century, which occupied a vacant barracks building.

Killis P. Almond Jr.'s 1981 Preservation Plan notes:

> *This two-story building was constructed as the base [post] movie theatre and has a rectangular plan with a gable roof. The walls are stuccoed structural clay tile with blind relief moldings which impanel the side and rear facades. The front (north) facade forms the lobby and has a metal marquee. The central wood ticket booth is flanked by two sets of ten-light French doors. The two outermost bays have arched openings and fanlight transoms. Pilasters support the returns of the raking wood cornice at the gable. The roof line is broken at the lobby and auditorium juncture, the larger gable parapet end having a blind lunette at the apex of the tympanum. The roof is covered with cement asbestos tile laid diagonally. The condition of the building is good. The front cornice at the northeast corner and the return has deteriorated and has been replaced with plain flat boards. The arched openings at the front have been boarded up with movie poster cabinets mounted on the boards. The stucco moldings have cracked and fallen off in some places. The metal gutters are also falling into disrepair.*

The post theater was erected in 1932 on the site of the nineteenth-century post hose house, a small frame storage building for firefighting equipment, followed in 1917 by a classic wartime YMCA building that was later converted to a service club. Panoramic photos from the 1920s show an outdoor screen set up behind the YMCA building so the soldiers could experience "moving picture shows."

This reminiscence of Abigail Robenson Boylan, of when she was an eight-year-old tomboy growing up at Fort Clark, sets the scene.

> *In the summer, the Post Theater [the YMCA in 1926] was uncomfortably hot. It was converted to an open air theater by having the movie projector cast its images through a window in the rear of the building onto an outdoor screen. The movies were silent that is all there was to it. The screen was supported by, and elevated on an escort wagon. Freeloaders were discouraged by a ten foot canvas curtain encompassing the theater patron's seats. The flaw in this arrangement was the space left between the bed of the wagon and the ground. An enterprising youngster could use the wagon wheels for*

Fort Clark's 1917 YMCA building, future site of the Post Theater. *Author's collection.*

Outdoor movie screen behind the YMCA building in 1925. *Author's collection.*

cover and slip into the enclosure undetected. This did not work for long, and one night I was apprehended by a trooper of the guard. In answer to my plea, to be allowed to stay, he firmly said, "Orders is orders." Luckily I was not reported for that infraction of regulations.

As the times changed, the army made a conscious effort to keep in step with American society by providing soldiers with modern recreation and entertainment facilities, often in a vain attempt to discourage soldiers from patronizing the seedier establishments in Brackettville. To serve that noble purpose, the Post Theater was built in 1932. Its design is the classic "movie house" Art Deco style of the 1930s, and it is the only steel-frame structure built by the army in the historic district. The theater featured refrigerated air (the new invention of Willis Carrier), lobby blackout curtains, a concession stand, compressed seaweed acoustical tile walls and seating for nearly four hundred soldiers.

Again, reference is made to the 1997 study of the U.S. Quartermaster General standardized plans, 1866–1942, by the Corps of Engineers, which summarizes the evolution and common architectural features of a post theater:

The Army began to build movie theaters at its installations as the movie industry evolved and became a popular form of entertainment. At first, older buildings were adapted for use as movie theaters. During the wave of new construction of the late 1920s and the 1930s, movie theaters became typical features of Army installations. Theaters were added to older installations and were standard components of new post plans. The construction of theaters reflected the Army's increasing concern with the well-being and morale of military personnel. Theaters were located within the heart of the cantonment area, near the barracks. The same basic plan was executed in both Georgian Colonial and Spanish Colonial Revival designs. U.S. Army movie theaters usually were one-story, rectangular, front-gabled buildings with long, unfenestrated side walls. The focus of the design was the front facade and entrance, which often featured a projecting vestibule or display marquee. Movie theaters on military installations did not display the ornate ornament of the civilian movie palaces of the same era. Most military movie theaters built for that purpose were brick buildings with simplified Georgian Colonial Revival or Spanish Mission Revival details. Theaters are associated with the growth of social and cultural amenities provided to military personnel during the late 1920s and 1930s and with the appearance of the movie industry. During the 1930s, movie theaters and athletic facilities provided the major sources of recreation and entertainment on installations.

The 5th, 112th, and 9th Cavalry bands all, in turn, frequently played outside in the evening to attract troopers to the show. The theater served the garrison for only twelve years before Fort Clark quietly and unceremoniously slipped into history and out of active service on August 28, 1944, when the last soldiers departed.

During the 1950s and 60s, after Brown and Root's purchase of the grounds from the U.S. government (through a Brown and Root subsidiary, the Texas Railway Equipment Company), the site was operated as the Fort Clark Guest Ranch. Starting in 1958, the Driskill Hotel of Austin managed the Guest Ranch operations. Sometime during this era, the theater's projection equipment, screen and seats were removed. The floor was terraced, but the stage area was retained.

In May 1971, the property was sold to a private developer who created a gated community and property owners association, which operates today as the Fort Clark Springs Association. The Post Theater was renamed the Town Hall and used for assemblies, dances and theatricals—in fact,

The Post Theater soon after completion, a classic U.S. Army movie house. *Author's collection.*

Popular 1930s linen postcard depicting the Post Theater. *Author's collection.*

Post Theater interior during the Guest Ranch era. *Author's collection.*

Evolutions of the Post Theater to include interior views. *Author's collection.*

everything but movies. The Post Theater was designated a Recorded Texas Historic Landmark in 1997 and was in use until recently for social events and by Fort Clark's Old Quarry Society for the Performing Arts for stage productions.

Fort Clark's Post Theater retains its architectural ornamentation, design features and exterior materials from the early 1930s. Character-defining features of the theater include the overall shape of the building, the ticket and lobby vestibules, the blank side and rear facades, the marquees and ornamentation on the front facade.

1932

NEW CAVALRY BARRACKS

Fort Clark's New Cavalry Barracks, Seminole Hall, today. *Photo by author.*

NEW CAVALRY BARRACKS

THE EARLIEST QUARTERS FOR SOLDIERS AT FORT CLARK WERE TENTS ALONG LAS MORAS CREEK NEAR THE SPRING. DURING THE FORT'S 1870s BUILDING BOOM, THREE CAVALRY BARRACKS WERE CONSTRUCTED, BUT BY THE LATE 1920s THEY HAD BECOME TOO DETERIORATED FOR CONTINUED USE. THREE TWO-STORY STONE CAVALRY BARRACKS WERE CONSTRUCTED 1931–1932 TO REPLACE THE THREE BARRACKS THAT WERE RAZED. THIS NEW, FOURTH BARRACKS WAS CONSTRUCTED ON THE SITE OF THE FIRST POST COMMISSARY WHICH HAD BURNED IN MARCH 1892, LEAVING THE SITE VACANT FOR FORTY YEARS. WHEN THE BUILDING WAS COMPLETED IT CONTAINED STATE OF THE ART FACILITIES, INCLUDING THREE 30 BY 65 FOOT OPEN BAYS FOR BUNKS AND WALL LOCKERS, A MESS HALL, TROOP OFFICES, SUPPLY AND ARMS ROOMS AND A LATRINE. THE BUILDING WAS SO MODERN AND IMPRESSIVE THAT IT WAS SINGLED OUT IN

ORDER TO JUSTIFY THE RETENTION OF FORT CLARK AS A PERMANENT MILITARY POST. THE FIRST OCCUPANTS OF THE BARRACKS WERE THE SOLDIERS OF "F" TROOP, 5TH U.S. CAVALRY. IN 1941 THE 5TH CAVALRY LEFT THE POST AND THE BARRACKS WERE USED BY THE 112TH CAVALRY OF THE TEXAS NATIONAL GUARD. THE BUFFALO SOLDIERS OF THE 9TH CAVALRY, AFRICAN AMERICAN TROOPS, MOVED INTO THE BARRACKS IN FALL 1942. LASTLY, FOR THE REMAINDER OF WORLD WAR II, THE BARRACKS WERE OCCUPIED BY 182 AFRICAN AMERICAN ENLISTED WOMEN OF THE WOMAN'S ARMY CORPS DETACHMENT OF THE 1855TH SERVICE UNIT. THE TWO-STORY RECTANGULAR PLAN BARRACKS IS BUILT ATOP A RAISED CONCRETE BASEMENT. LOAD-BEARING WALLS ARE OF LIMESTONE WEBWALL CONSTRUCTION, WITH CAST STONE WINDOW SILLS AND STEEL LINTELS. THE MAIN ELEVATION IS DIVIDED INTO FIFTEEN BAYS BY SQUARE WOODEN COLUMNS, WITH A CROSS-BRACED RAILING ALONG THE SECOND-STORY PORCH.
—RTHL, 2009

Fort Clark's New Cavalry Barracks building served as quarters for enlisted men and women of the fort's garrison from 1932 to 1944. The building is recognized in the National Register narrative as a contributing structure to the Fort Clark Historic District. This distinctive building was home for soldiers of America's Greatest Generation.

As noted by Killis P. Almond Jr. in his 1981 Fort Clark Historic District Preservation Plan,

This two story structure has a rectangular plan and a hipped roof. The walls are of common faced limestone webwall with cast stone window sills and hidden steel lintels. There is a raised foundation of concrete with a full basement. The front (south) porch is divided into fifteen bays divided by individual solid wood square columns. The second floor has a crossed braced two by four railing. The porch roof is continuous with the main roof and hipped at the returns. Window sash is typically six over six double hung and doors have glass lites, the roof is asbestos cement shingling. The building is in very good condition. The original beaded pointing and stone work is in good condition.

Not until 1870 did permanent quarters for soldiers exist on Fort Clark. Two single-story infantry barracks were built of stone that year by the Buffalo Soldiers of the 25th Infantry. By 1874, the fort's garrison had grown to regimental size, requiring the largest construction effort in the fort's existence, during which four single-story infantry barracks and three two-story cavalry barracks, all of stone, were completed. The infantry barracks survive as private homes. The cavalry barracks met a different fate. By 1928, they were in such a serious state of deterioration that the inspector general recommended costly and extensive repairs be made. Subsequently, two of these barracks were replaced in 1931 on the footprints of the 1874 buildings and joined to the single-story, circa-1886 rear support buildings to create a *U* shape. Both buildings were constructed of hollow tile brick with a limestone veneer. In 1932, construction began to replace the third 1874 cavalry barracks. At that time, a decision was made to build a fourth cavalry barracks, significantly larger and a major departure in design from the other three.

This new cavalry barracks would occupy the site of the first post commissary lost to fire on March 31, 1892, on ground that had been vacant for forty years. When completed, the barracks was state-of-the-art troop billeting with three thirty-by-sixty-five-foot open bays for bunks and wall lockers with hardwood floors and beaded board ceilings; a self-contained mess hall; and a full basement for troop offices, a supply room, an arms room and a latrine for one hundred men, all under one roof.

When Fort Clark was threatened with closure in the early 1930s, a locally produced pamphlet expounded on the modern facilities that justified keeping Fort Clark open. So modern and impressive was this building that it was used as one of the reasons to substantiate the retention of Fort Clark as a permanent military post.

> *The housing capacity of Fort Clark is sufficient to accommodate nine hundred enlisted men and sixty officers. The majority of the barracks and houses are constructed of stone. Recently, however, two new two story barracks have been erected. These new barracks are sufficient to house one troop each. They were built at an approximate cost of Two Hundred Dollars per man housed. The material used in the construction of these barracks is hollow tile, veneered stone finish, concrete flooring and asphalt shingle roofs, which is the most durable type of construction known.*

The first occupants were the soldiers of F Troop, 5th U.S. Cavalry, who justly earned their reputation as the best troop in the regiment and now had the finest, most modern barracks on the post. The 5th Cavalry departed Fort Clark in early 1941, replaced by the 112th Cavalry of the Texas National Guard. Next came the Buffalo Soldiers of the 9th Cavalry in the summer of 1942. Finally, the barracks was home to the 182 Black enlisted women of the Woman's Army Corps Detachment of the 1855th Service Unit during World War II.

The New Cavalry Barracks interior in 1932. *Author's collection.*

Troop F, 5th Cavalry in front of their new barracks in the 1930s. *Author's collection.*

A picture postcard of the New Cavalry Barracks in 1940. *Author's collection.*

The new cavalry barracks served the garrison for only twelve years and has seen little effective use since Fort Clark closed and was sold in 1946. In the early days of the Fort Clark Springs Association, the building was used as a youth center and the basement for commodities distribution. Now open only two days a year, during Fort Clark Days, the building remains a strong candidate for adaptive reuse as a hostel or unique military history–themed lodging; the only thing lacking is a vision.

Fort Clark's New Cavalry Barracks is a classic and enduring example of army architecture from the early 1930s with what is perhaps a one-of-a-kind design to suit the specific location of the building. Of the four two-story cavalry barracks remaining in the Fort Clark Historic District, two have experienced irreversible unsympathetic modifications to create motel units and a third is used for offices by the property owners association. Only this barracks, now called Seminole Hall, stands alone as essentially unaltered. The New Cavalry Barracks is the finest example of twentieth-century soldier housing in the Fort Clark Historic District. This building may well be one of only a handful of pre–World War II stone barracks left on any army post in the nation and perhaps the sole remaining example of this type of military architecture in Texas.

1932

U.S. ARMY SIGNAL CORPS BUILDING

Fort Clark's U.S. Army Signal Corps Building, today a comfortable home. *Photo by author.*

U.S. ARMY SIGNAL CORPS BUILDING

THIS BUILDING SERVED AS THE COMMUNICATIONS CENTER FOR FORT CLARK FROM 1932–1944. THE BUILDING IS OF TILE BRICK CONSTRUCTION WITH A VENEER OF IRREGULAR CUT FIELD STONE. THE ORIGINAL FOOTPRINT WAS ENLARGED C. 1940 TO ACCOMMODATE BARRACKS FOR ENLISTED SOLDIERS. DURING WORLD WAR II MOBILIZATION, THE 3RD SIGNAL TROOP OF THE 2ND CAVALRY DIVISION AND THE SIGNAL DETACHMENT OF THE 1855TH SERVICE COMPANY SHARED THIS BUILDING AND MAINTAINED THE POST TELEPHONE SYSTEM, ARMY TRAINING FILM LIBRARY, POST PHOTO LAB, AND OTHER ESSENTIAL EQUIPMENT. THE SIGNAL CORPS DETACHMENT WERE THE LAST TROOPS TO LEAVE FORT CLARK WHEN IT CLOSED ON AUGUST 28, 1944.

—RTHL, 2008

Fort Clark's U.S. Army Signal Corps building served as the Communications Center for the garrison from 1932 to 1944. The building is recognized in the National Register narrative as a contributing structure to the Fort Clark Historic District. This unique special-purpose building was once home to soldiers of the fort's Signal Corps detachment.

As noted by Killis P. Almond Jr. in his 1981 Fort Clark Historic District Preservation Plan,

> *This one story stone veneer house has a rectangular plan with a hipped roof. Stonework is webwall with cast stone window sills. Six over six double hung wood sash windows are typical. The roof is cement asbestos shingles laid diagonally. The house is in excellent condition, with few alterations being evident from the exterior.*

Fort Clark's earliest recorded "signal" accomplishment was the first telegraph line from the fort to the Menger Hotel in San Antonio, completed by Second Lieutenant William Paulding of the 10th Infantry in September 1875. A Signal Corps detachment was first assigned to Fort Clark in January 1906. From that date, the Signal Corps was vital "permanent party" for the garrison. Advances in military signal communications from the original telegraph to carrier pigeons, the telephone, the radio and radio teletype saw the Signal Corps play an increasingly important role in life on the post and its contact with the outside world—so much so that, ultimately, the signal detachment required a standalone facility to efficiently perform its function.

In the years leading up to World War II, the importance of rapid communications was recognized and massive strides made in the development of communications equipment. Rather than being an adjunct to other signal corps functions, specialized facilities were needed to house this equipment and the personnel trained in its use.

Fort Clark's signal building carried building number 95 during its army service. Construction was carried out in two phases, beginning in 1931–32 when the post experienced a number of major construction projects. Construction is tile brick veneered with an irregular cut fieldstone and a plain mortar joint, the same style as other permanent buildings built on the fort during the 1930s.

The first phase of the building was a basic rectangle measuring fifty-five by thirty feet. This apparently proved inadequate for the intended purpose, and the building was extended an additional twenty feet to accommodate a barracks/dormitory area for the enlisted soldiers of the Signal Corps

Fort Clark's signal building in 1937. *Author's collection.*

detachment, who could now also live where they worked. The date of the addition is estimated to be circa 1940, based on available data. The 1937 photo above does not show the addition; however, the circa 1944 photo on the following page does. There is also a small (approximately ten-by-twelve-foot) building in the rear, which housed auxiliary power equipment to provide emergency electrical power. The 1937 photo further indicates that this building was also used as a meteorological data collection point for the fort, as there are weather instruments visible mounted on a rooftop platform.

It is not known where the fort's communications function was located prior to completion of this new facility. What can be surmised, however, is that the former location was likely inadequate for several reasons. At this time, the radio and radio teletype systems were in common use in the army and required shelter and corresponding space for the supporting antenna systems. The new site behind the officers' row of houses could both accommodate the enormous radio sets of the day and allow adequate space for an antenna farm. The antenna foundations remain in place behind the west side of the building, as do the antenna tie-down guys, the elevation marking plate and the underground cable access, complete with U.S. Signal Corps manhole cover, that fed the antenna and power cables into the building. All available

The rear of Fort Clark's signal building is shown in this 1944 image taken from an antenna tower. *Author's collection.*

photos of this building were taken from an elevated point from the southwest corner of the building, probably from one of the antennas, as there are no elevated points in the area.

During the World War II mobilization in 1943–44, the 3rd Signal Troop of the 2nd Cavalry Division and the Signal Detachment of the 1855th Service Company shared this building and maintained the post telephone system, the army training film library, the post photo lab and all other essential communications equipment within its walls and grounds. The signal building served the garrison for only twelve years until Fort Clark quietly and unceremoniously slipped into history and out of active service on August 28, 1944; some of the last soldiers to depart were from the Signal Corps Detachment.

Today, the building has been adapted for use as family housing and its exterior sympathetically altered by the filling in with native stone of two door openings and a window and the addition of front and rear porches and a carport. All these minor modifications were accomplished using original construction methods and materials in order to retain, to the greatest extent possible, the original configuration and overall appearance.

As a special-purpose service support building, the signal building ranks equally with the hospital, commissary, motor pool and stables as a crucial post facility, performing the unique essential function of managing the communications and information systems support for the command and control of the garrison. This building may well be one of only a handful of signal corps facilities remaining from the "quiet time" between World Wars I and II on any army post in the nation.

1938

ARMY SERVICE CLUB

Fort Clark's Army Service Club today. *Photo by author.*

Fort Clark's Army Service Club building served as a morale and welfare facility for the fort's garrison from 1938 to 1944. The building is recognized in the National Register narrative as a compatible structure to the Fort Clark Historic District. This unique special-purpose building was a place of rest and relaxation for soldiers of America's Greatest Generation.

One of the earliest definitive reflections on the off-duty pursuits of soldiers at Fort Clark appears in the memoirs of Lieutenant William Paulding, 10th Infantry, in which he observes that, in 1875, "their amusements were only baseball and hunting, so that at night they visited the town of Brackettville which was full of rum holes and gambling dens and crude women....There were no places of amusement such as they have these days, so what could one expect? Nothing."

Just over a decade later, in 1887, a vacant infantry barracks was converted to use as a post hall where theatricals and concerts were presented. The officers and ladies of the 19th Infantry and the 8th Cavalry performed *The Mikado* at the post hall on February 8 and 11, 1887. In addition, as the nineteenth century drew to a close, Fort Clark made a conscious effort to keep in step with American society by providing the soldiers with another modern recreation facility, transforming a second infantry barracks into a gymnasium. By the beginning of the twentieth century, the only remaining jacal mess hall (see chapter 2), circa 1870, had been converted to use as an amusement hall, according to the 1904 post map.

However, there still was no real place where a soldier could just relax, unwind, write a letter home or socialize outside a barracks full of noisy troopers. Credit goes to the YMCA for originating the service club concept at Fort Clark during the mobilization for World War I. Corporal Maynard McKinnon, Ambulance Company No. 7, wrote to his fiancée on November 28, 1917,

> *You asked about the Y.M.C.A. Well you can see by this it is finished and open. Opened last Sat. eve but this is the first chance I have had to use it. And believe me it does help a lot and makes things cheerful. Right now the piano is going & I have been sitting looking into the fireplace and dreaming of you.*

The YMCA building occupied the future site of the Post Theater, which was built in 1932 and designated an RTHL in 1997.

The Service Club occupies the site of the first post guard house, on the prominent ridge overlooking Las Moras Creek and the bridge leading onto the fort. The building was constructed in 1938 by Taini Construction of Del Rio, Texas, with Phillip Garoni acting as site supervisor (the next year, this same company built Dickman Hall.

As noted by Killis P. Almond Jr. in his 1981 Fort Clark Historic District Preservation Plan,

> *This one story structure has a rectangular plan with gabled roofs. The foundation is limestone webwall with a wood frame superstructure sheathed with horizontal siding. Windows are typically wood four by four casement. A stone porch adjoins the front entrance at the east façade. The south wall has a wood frame extension with a hipped roof which returns to the south wall of the body of the building. Between the higher gabled roof and extension roof are a series of stepped wood louvered vents.*

Now enlisted soldiers once again had a place to "get away from it all," a place where they could relax and write letters or read a magazine, play pool or just have a cup of coffee. An interior photo of the building shows lounge chairs around the fireplace and reflects a homey, nonmilitary atmosphere. During the World War II mobilization in 1943–44, the building's use became more exclusive, as it was reserved for noncommissioned officers. However, this NCO club was restricted to White soldiers only and excluded the Buffalo

Army Service Club during World War II. *Author's collection.*

Rare view of the interior of the Service Club in its army days. *Author's collection.*

Guest Ranch era use as a country club. *Author's collection.*

Soldiers of the 2nd Cavalry Division also stationed at Fort Clark at the time. The Service Club building served the garrison for only seven years until Fort Clark was closed in 1944. It was during the Guest Ranch era, 1950–71, that the building served as a country club facility for the Brackettville community. Fond memories still linger of the wonderful meals, dances and well-attended parties many experienced there.

The Army Service Club on Fort Clark is a classic and enduring example of army frame construction architecture from the late 1930s, with perhaps a one-of-a-kind design to suit the specific location of the building. The building is still in use, serving its original intended purpose as a rest and relaxation facility. The Fort Clark Springs Association makes use of the building for social functions and gatherings. The nostalgic simplicity and the distinctive look of the building's shiplap siding and plentiful windows, painted in the post color scheme of light gray, ivory cream and seal brown, at once recall not only the quiet time of the prewar years but also the excitement of the mobilization for World War II.

As a special-purpose service support building, the Service Club ranks equally with the signal corps building, post hospital, commissary, motor pool and stables as a crucial post facility, performing the unique essential function of providing for soldiers' morale and welfare. This building may well be one of only a handful of pre–World War II frame service club facilities remaining on any army post in the nation.

1939

OFFICERS' CLUB OPEN MESS

Fort Clark's Officers' Club Open Mess today. *Photo by author.*

OFFICERS' CLUB OPEN MESS

THIS BUILDING SERVED FORT CLARK FROM 1939 TO 1944 AND WAS NAMED "DICKMAN HALL" AFTER CAREER CAVALRY OFFICER MAJ. GEN. JOSEPH T. DICKMAN (1857–1927). THE GROUND FLOOR HOUSED A LOUNGE, DINING ROOM, TAP ROOM, KITCHEN, GUEST ROOM, MAID'S ROOM AND FOUR ROOMS FOR VISITING OFFICERS. THE SECOND FLOOR HELD A SPACIOUS BALLROOM. THE TWO-STORY BUILDING HAS A MAIN HIPPED ROOF WITH GABLE ROOFED BAYS FLANKING A CENTRAL ARCHED PORTICO ENTRANCE. A WEBWALL STONE VENEER CLADS FRAME AND CLAY TILE CONSTRUCTION. THE BUILDING LATER BECAME GUEST RANCH HEADQUARTERS AND THEN A RESTAURANT AND LOUNGE FOR THE FORT CLARK SPRINGS ASSOCIATION.

—RTHL, 2010

Fort Clark's Dickman Hall served as the post officers' club and open mess from 1939 to 1944. The building is recognized in the National Register narrative as a contributing structure to the Fort Clark Historic District. This distinctive building was the officers' club for the 5th Cavalry Regiment, the 112th Cavalry Regiment, the 9th Cavalry Regiment and the 2nd Cavalry Division. The presence of this building is conclusively linked to Fort Clark's significant contribution to United States Army heritage.

The National Register narrative notes,

> *Twentieth century construction on the fort continued to acknowledge the abundance of locally available stone although the method of construction varied from that of the earlier buildings. Erected in 1915* [1939] *in the northwest corner of the parade configuration, the noncommissioned* [Officers'] *Club is built with a frame structure veneered with an irregular cut field stone and a tooled mortar joint.* [Note: The 1979 narrative got the purpose of the building and the date wrong—even though the building has a 1939 cornerstone—but correctly identified the construction technique.]

The need for a building reserved exclusively for officers, where they could take their meals and socialize, evolved from long-established military traditions. A mess is the place where military personnel socialize, eat and (in some cases) live. The root of *mess* is the Old French *mes*, "portion of food," drawn from the Latin verb *mittere*, meaning "to send" or "to put," the original sense being "a course of a meal put on the table." This sense of *mess*, which appeared in English in the thirteenth century, was often used for cooked or liquid dishes in particular, as in the "mess of pottage" (porridge or soup) for which Esau in Genesis traded his birthright. By the fifteenth century, a group of people who ate together was also known as a *mess*, and it is this sense that was intended in the *mess halls* of the twentieth-century U.S. Army. The term has since been replaced by the bland identifier *dining facility*.

In the United States Army, officers historically have had to purchase their own food, using funds allocated to each officer. At the far-flung frontier posts of the West, such as Fort Clark, officers would organize their food service in two ways. A closed mess was when the few officers of a small garrison would pool all their funds to provide all meals only to the members—thus being "closed" to outsiders, except guests. At a larger post, the greater pool of officers would allow officers to purchase meals on an individual meal basis (after payment of a small monthly dues amount). Such arrangements were called open messes.

The closed mess was more a practice of the nineteenth-century army and flourished at Fort Clark, as noted in regular diary entries by Lieutenant Francis Henry French, E Company, 19th Infantry, who served at Fort Clark from 1882 to 1887.

> *April 12, 1884—Capt. Hall & family joined our mess again today on account of the departure of their cook, a most welcome addition to our mess. Dined & joined Crowder's mess, Scott being present with Crowder; Gorgas is other member. One man runs it a month, taking turns. Mess includes all necessary expenses, house laundry & eating. Hope to save money.*
>
> *April 30, 1888—After tattoo went down to the officer' club room. This was originally the storeroom for condemned property but Gardener* [Cornelius Gardener, USMA 1873, First Lieutenant, 19th Infantry] *had transformed it into a beautiful suite of rooms and it makes a very pleasant place to pass an evening.*

The open mess concept at Fort Clark is first documented on a post map that identifies quarters No. 6–7 as the "Officers' Mess" in 1915. The site of the future Officers' Club is also recorded on this same map as the ruin of the Post Trader's store. In 1939, this site of the first post commissary and quartermaster storehouse, on the prominent ridge overlooking Las Moras

Fort Clark's 1850s quartermaster storehouse converted to bachelor officer quarters in the 1930s, the future site of Dickman Hall. *Author's collection.*

Creek and the bridge leading onto the fort, was chosen as the location for the new Officers' Club. The building was constructed by Taini Construction of Del Rio, Texas, with Phillip Garoni acting as site supervisor.

As noted by Killis P. Almond Jr. in his 1981 Fort Clark Historic District Preservation Plan description of the building,

> *This two story building has a rectangular plan with a main hipped roof with gable roofed bays which flank a central (south) entrance. This building is webwall stone veneer with structural clay tile backing constructed during the 1930s as the officers club. The central entrance is in the form of a three bay arched stone portico with a deck above. Windows are typically ten by ten, four by four, and three by three wood casements. The condition of the building is very good. This is the only twentieth century building within the district which exhibits a degree of stone craftsmanship equal to the earlier buildings. The walls are webwall, but highlighted at the windows with solid stone flat lintels and solid voussoirs at the arched portico. The roof is now covered with asphalt composition shingles.*

This noble stone building bears the name Dickman Hall, carved in the stone above the entrance arch by the United States Army when the building was built to serve as the Officers' Club for the 5th U.S. Cavalry Regiment. The building's namesake, Major General Joseph T. Dickman, served at Fort Clark as a lieutenant in the 3rd Cavalry from 1887 to 1892. A West Point graduate, class of 1881, Dickman's eminent forty-five-year military career included service in the Geronimo Campaign, the Spanish-American War, the Philippine Insurrection, the Boxer Rebellion, the Peking Relief Expedition and World War I. He commanded the 2nd Cavalry Regt 1915–17; the 85th Infantry Division, the 3rd Infantry Division, I Corps, and Third Army in World War I; and the Southern Department and VIII Corps Area (1919–21). Dickman retired on October 6, 1921, and died in Washington, D.C., on October 24, 1927. To the officers of the 5th Cavalry at Fort Clark, their new officers' club was fittingly named for a most notable and popular cavalryman, Major General Joseph T. Dickman.

On the eve of World War II, the new club was an imposing structure: spacious, well-appointed with modern conveniences and decorated in the Art Deco style of the era. "The Club" quickly became the pride of the officer corps (and, more probably, the pride of the officers' wives) on the post and the focal point of social activities for the officer class. As evidenced by the original floor plans, the ground floor archways were all open, forming the porch entrance. A lounge, dining room, taproom, kitchen, guest room, maid's room and four rooms for visiting officers' quarters occupied the first floor. The second floor featured an airy ballroom with a hardwood dance floor, the only such amenity for miles around. Countless parties were held here by the officers of the 5th Cavalry, 112th Cavalry, 9th Cavalry, and 2nd Cavalry Division. It was a place of genuine memories and good times.

As the fort passed into civilian ownership, the building continued to perform its original intended purpose, taking on a decided elegance during the twenty-five years of the Brown and Root Guest Ranch era. Period photos reflect the style and class typical of Guest Ranch adaptive reuse of army facilities, which always tastefully complemented the already historic setting.

The Officers' Club served the garrison for only five years, until Fort Clark was retired from active service on August 28, 1944. The Fort Clark Guest Ranch used Dickman Hall as a dining room and lounge, and it became Ranch Headquarters in 1959, when the old Post Headquarters building was destroyed by fire. In 1971, the building was again put to use by the property owners association as a restaurant and lounge, until 2004, when it was closed.

The Officers' Club Open Mess at Fort Clark is a classic and enduring example of twentieth-century army architecture, with a distinctive, one-of-a-kind design. Today, over eighty years later, the building sits relatively dormant, out of full use for a generation. Of the twentieth-century buildings remaining in the Fort Clark Historic District, this is the most prominent,

Officers' Club Open Mess time capsule and interior views during the Guest Ranch era. *Author's collection.*

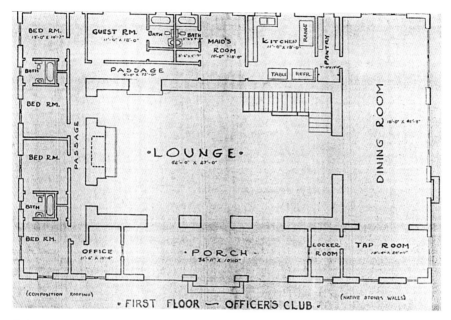

Officers' Club Open Mess first-floor plan, 1939. *Author's collection.*

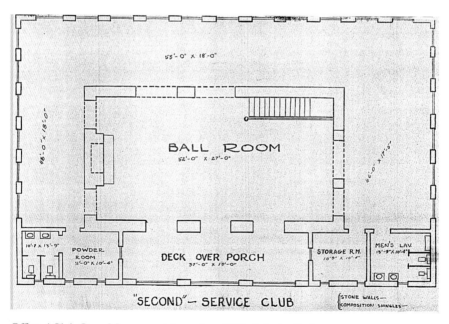

Officers' Club Open Mess second-floor plan, 1939. *Author's collection.*

and it awaits rejuvenation as a polished jewel in the crown of the Fort Clark National Register Historic District—and, indeed, the nation.

As a special-purpose building, the Officers' Club ranks equally with the post hospital, commissary, motor pool and stables as a crucial post facility, performing the unique essential function of serving the officers of the garrison. This building may well be one of only a handful of "Officers' Club" facilities remaining from the "quiet time" between World Wars I and II on any army post in the nation and perhaps the only such example of this type of unique military architecture in Texas.

PART III

THE TWENTY-FIRST CENTURY

RECOGNIZED HISTORIC FEATURES,

PEOPLE AND EVENTS

Tangible acknowledgements of Fort Clark's significant history and service to the nation in the form of official Texas Historical Markers, privately funded plaques, interpretive signage and local markers informing the visiting public of the prominent role Fort Clark has played in the shaping of Texas history were slow to appear. The three historical medallions awarded in the early '60s for the Guard House, Palisado Building and Wainwright House all disappeared without a trace and were not replaced with standard RTHL interpretive markers for over thirty years. In the case of the Palisado Building, it took over forty-five years for a replacement marker to be issued.

In the 1990s, through the efforts of pioneer researchers Don Swanson, Ben Pingenot and B. Peter Pohl, RTHL markers were awarded for the Patton House, the Officers' Row Quarters and the Post Theater. Ben secured the first THC subject marker, "Fort Clark," in 1994, and the Brackett High School History Club, under the mentorship of Kathy Bader, secured another subject marker for the "Seminole Scout Camp on Fort Clark" in 2002. Three more subject markers have since been awarded through the THC's Undertold Stories Program: 2nd Cavalry Division at Fort Clark (2010), Las Moras Spring (2013) and John Horse (2014). The Undertold Stories Program is a specially funded THC initiative that proactively documents significant underrepresented subjects or untold stories in Texas. After a rigorous annual statewide application process, if a subject qualifies and is selected, the marker is provided at no cost. To have three of these markers is indeed a rare achievement for such a small private community as Fort

The Empty Saddle statue, emblematic of Fort Clark's active service, 1852–1944. *Photo by author.*

Las Moras Spring subject marker 2013, at the post swimming pool. *Photo by author.*

Clark Springs. One other subject marker was awarded in 2011 for the Site of Original Post Cemetery. For rich detail on all these markers, please visit the Historical Marker Database at www.HMdb.org and simply enter the name of the marker in the search bar.

Interpretive signage, when compatible with NPS standards, can communicate additional information not available on historical markers by including more detailed text, dynamic graphics and historic images that better serve to enhance visitors' perceptions and knowledge of a site. Fort Clark's Historic District currently has four interpretive signage locations to serve that purpose: at the Post Theater, to complement the district walking tour, placed by the Fort Clark Historical Society; at the post flagpole, detailing the service of the 2nd Cavalry Division, placed during the Last Tattoo of the Buffalo Soldiers, a reunion of veterans of the 2nd Cavalry Division held at Fort Clark in 2008 and again in 2010; in Rendezvous Park, describing the 1840 fight at Las Moras Spring, placed by the Friends of the Fort Clark Historic District; and in front of the 1857 Post Headquarters building, recognizing the sesquicentennial of Mackenzie's Remolino Raid, placed by the Fort Clark Heritage Council.

While awaiting the official recognition of a Texas Historical Marker, several of Fort Clark's historic buildings have received National Register

Fight at Las Moras Spring signage and monument in Rendezvous Park. *Photo by author.*

Station Hospital and its National Register plaque. *Photo by author.*

plaques placed by individuals and organizations to honor their identity and origins as U.S. Army structures: the 1854 Powder Magazine; the 1930s Station Hospital; the 1874 Post Forage House, Granary and Bakery; and the 1939 Motor Pool Dormitory. There are also National Register plaques displayed for Quarters No. 2–3 and 4, Married Officers' Quarters No. 8–9 and Officers' Row Quarters No. 25–26.

Local historical markers serve to satisfy the need for recognition when a site or event would not otherwise qualify for the state marker program. It goes without saying that a local historical marker should never be homemade but should strive to replicate formal official markers. Bronze and aluminum markers communicate with dignity and class the refinement of the organization sponsoring the marker. I was the first to facilitate the Fort Clark Historical Society's sponsorship of a local marker for the Forsyth Bridge in 1995. The next year, a marker to commemorate the dual anniversary of fifty years since the closure of Fort Clark and twenty-five years since the chartering of the Fort Clark Springs Association was installed at the Member Services building by the property owners association. In 2004, on the twenty-fifth anniversary of its founding, the Fort Clark Historical Society placed a large bronze roadside marker at the entrance to the National Register Historic District. In 2009, a bronze

Left: Forsyth Bridge marker dedication by "The Colonel's Daughter," Elizabeth Forsyth Scheuber, in 1995. *Photo by author.*

Below: U.S. Army Unit Memorial. *Photo by author.*

plaque honoring Juan Avila was mounted and dedicated by Fort Clark Springs at the post motor pool to recognize his fifty-six years of service to Fort Clark and rededicate the facility in his name.

On Memorial Day 2005, the Fort Clark Historical Society broke ground for a distinctive monument honoring the United States Army units that served at Fort Clark, Texas, from its establishment in June 1852 until the post closed on August 28, 1944. Four custom bronze plaques list, by branch, these units and also recognize Medal of Honor recipients who served at Fort Clark. The memorial also immortalizes the Seminole-Negro Indian

Scouts, Fort Clark's longest-serving unit, with plaques listing the names of all the scouts. The site was deeded to the Fort Clark Historical Society that same year. This ambitious project was my concept and carried out under my diligent leadership, direction and energy. Over the next five years, nearly $12,000 was raised, entirely through the generosity of local citizens, so a total of eight bronze plaques could be designed, purchased and installed at the site. The Seminole-Negro Indian Scout Detachment plaques were dedicated on September 17, 2005, in conjunction with the annual Seminole Day celebration held in Brackettville by descendants of the scouts. The stone pedestals are surrounded by an island of memorial bricks. It should be noted that the flagpole has been removed from the unit marker pedestal and replaced by a statue of a White World War II infantryman. It is an irrefutable historic fact that not a single White infantryman served at Fort Clark during World War II. However, nearly ten thousand Black cavalrymen did serve proudly at Fort Clark in World War II. The reader may be the judge of whether the service of these last of the Buffalo Soldiers is honored by this most inappropriate statue.

THE REAR RANK

OTHER HISTORIC U.S. ARMY STRUCTURES AND SITES

Charles C. Perkins, a private in Company K, 1st Massachusetts Infantry Regiment, in the years following his Civil War service, was known to refer to himself as HPRR, which meant "High Private of the Rear Ranks." The phrase is intended to describe a soldier who quietly performs his duties, uncomplaining, without much notice or recognition. Nonetheless, such a soldier's service is honorable, reliable and often noteworthy. The rear rank also has similar numbers as the front rank. So it is that Fort Clark's yet-to-be-recognized historic buildings constitute a rear rank of history and U.S. Army architecture of equal merit and numbers as those currently honored with Recorded Texas Historic Landmark designations.

These overlooked yet highly qualified candidates for RTHL designation are here divided into three groups: those owned by the Fort Clark Springs Association, those in private ownership and those owned by a local government. For the majority of these buildings, there is rich detail existing about their individual history to be drawn from maps, photographs, inspection reports and, in several cases, the actual Quartermaster Department plans retained in the National Archives. In addition, almost all are described in Killis P. Almond Jr.'s 1981 Preservation Plan and included in the 1928 Inspection Report if built before that year.

There are, however, several obstacles to overcome in order for these candidates to gain the worthwhile and prestigious distinction of RTHL status. First are the persistent misconceptions and misinformation about Texas Historical Markers. Years ago, I encouraged the owners of Fort

Clark's 1885 Bachelor Hall to apply for RTHL designation, for which the building is eminently qualified. I was met with a firm, unwavering *no*, because the owners were convinced they would then be required to allow people into their home—pure hogwash, or any other synonym for "absolute nonsense" you may choose. Typically, only a change of ownership has the potential to reverse this deeply rooted mistaken belief. Such a pity people are so gullible; however, I guess politicians depend on it. Second, the property owner must have an informed willingness to pursue a marker application and subsequently pay for the marker. Third, the property itself must be in a good state of repair, responsibly maintained and not subject to unsympathetic changes to the historic character or appearance of the building. Under Texas law, RTHL owners are eligible for a 25 percent reduction in the appraised value of their property for property taxes as an incentive to encourage conscientious preservation.

The Fort Clark Springs Association owns thirteen basically unaltered U.S. Army historic structures that would be considered eligible for RTHL designation. The properties are listed here, with a brief history, in the order of their date of construction:

QUARTERMASTER CORRAL, 1870s: The original stone walls remain on the west and south sides, along with the stone Quartermaster Department (QMD) corral office (post building No. 90) on the southwest corner and another square rock structure (post building No. 88) on the southeast corner. The QMD office building is still in use. The stone walls were once the rear elevation of frame sheds where wagons were parked. At one time, the site was a completely walled enclosure and home to mules and escort wagons. This feature has often been falsely referred to as the "old fort," becoming yet another victim of Fort Clark's regrettably fractured history.

FORAGE HOUSE, 1870s: Post building No. 45. Over time, post maps identify this building first as a forage house, then as a granary and finally as a bakery in 1944. The building served as the sales offices for the Fort Clark Springs Association in the 1970s and then as home to the Fort Clark Community Council.

ICE HOUSE, 1880s: Post building No. 50. Fort Clark's first ice plant, later used as a butcher shop during its army service. This small, square stone building has retained its basic historic appearance, considering it is not in use and neglected.

QUARTERMASTER STOREHOUSE/COMMISSARY, 1892: Post building No. 74. This structure is by far the most architecturally significant building within the district and the greater area (Killis Almond). This building was built by local master stonemason James Cornell at a cost of $9,426.72 and replaced a previous quartermaster storehouse lost to fire on March 31, 1892. Today, this magnificent example of one-of-a-kind U.S. Army architecture sits empty, even though comprehensive plans for adaptive reuse exist.

AIR FIELD HANGAR, 1921: Post building No. 288. Fort Clark's Army Air Service hangar, built in 1921, is possibly the third-oldest military hangar in the nation and a classic example of the U.S. Army all-steel hangar, which was a workhorse design of the World War I era. This type of hangar was, in fact, mass-produced during the Great War, but many building components did not reach their intended locations until after the armistice, as is the case with Fort Clark's hangar. Once home to the 111th Observation Squadron in the "quiet time" between World War I and World War II, the airfield also had a weather station and two sets of enlisted quarters. In 1941, when the 112th Cavalry garrisoned the post, dances were frequently held in the hangar. Over the years, the hangar has suffered extensive hail damage, which has never been repaired. The building is an outlier of the historic district.

TENNIS COURT, 1925: A tennis court has occupied this site since the 1880s and was always a favorite form of recreation for the officer class, who enjoyed its exclusive use. Today it sits dormant and in decay, with little or no attention given to its original purpose.

STATION HOSPITAL, 1930s: Post building No. 60. This building is Fort Clark's third hospital and is built on the footprint of the 1873 hospital, which occupied the site for nearly fifty years. According to Killis Almond, it is evident that the millwork of the porches was reused from the nineteenth-century hospital for this twentieth-century replacement. Several unique features of this more modern hospital include an attached mess hall with a basement morgue, a detention ward with barred windows for sick prisoners, a maternity ward, private rooms for sick officers, a pharmacy, a dentist's office and a ward nurse's station. It is presently used as an adult recreation center by the property owners association. Recognition of its historic relationships is noticeably absent.

FIRE STATION, 1930s: Post building No. 199. This building includes three bays for fire trucks, a dormitory for soldier firemen, a large kitchen and latrine and rooms for noncommissioned officers. The Kinney County Volunteer Fire Department and EMS used this building for many years. The building is no longer in use.

CAVALRY BARRACKS, 1931: Post building No. 30. This building was built on the footprint of an 1874 cavalry barracks and has an incised limestone cornerstone dated 1931. During its army service, it was the home of Headquarters Troop, 1ˢᵗ Cavalry Brigade. One wing connected to the main building was formerly an 1886 mess hall and is now in use as the Fort Clark Springs Association boardroom. The other wing is longer and once served as a post exchange. The structure now houses the administrative offices of the property owners association.

MAIN ENTRANCE GATE, 1937–38: A popular subject for postcards, the entrance gate on U.S. Highway 90—with its distinctive stone pillars capped with large lanterns, featuring distinctive iron shields emblazoned with "Fort Clark," and gently curving stone walls—is nearly identical to the Ogden Gate at Fort Riley, Kansas. An incised stone paver in the sidewalk makes known the builder and construction date: "Q.M.C. 1937–38." The small, easily overlooked National Register plaque presented by the National Park Service is mounted on one of the stone pillars.

STABLES, 1939: Post building No. 51. Cavalry stables have occupied this site since 1870. Built in 1939 for Headquarters Troop, 1ˢᵗ Cavalry Brigade, these stables consist of two stone buildings—one used as a tack shed, the other as a blacksmith shop—connected by a span of covered stalls. Fort Clark's historic stables thrived during the Guest Ranch era and are still in use for their intended purpose.

POST SWIMMING POOL, 1939: Post building No. 294. There has been a swimming pool at this site since as early as 1902. The present swimming pool was built by the Works Progress Administration (WPA) and is the third-largest spring-fed pool in Texas, surpassed only by Balmorhea and Barton Springs. It is also the largest swimming pool ever built on any post in the army. As George S. Patton Jr. wrote to his wife, Beatrice, in the summer of 1938, "All one can do here is to Ride-Read-Write & Swim." By far the most popular feature of Fort Clark Springs and forever a jewel in the crown of

Primary FCSA-owned RTHL candidates: QMD Corral (*top, left*); Motor Pool (*top, right*); Commissary (*center*); Hospital (*bottom, left*); and Post Swimming Pool (*bottom, right*). *Author's collection.*

the historic district, it is more than deserving of recognition as a Recorded Texas Historic Landmark.

MOTOR POOL, 1939: Post building No. 168. A modernized version of the QMD corral, this building occupies ground set aside for exclusive use of the Quartermaster Department since the 1870s. The north side has open bays for motor vehicle storage, while the south side features open bays, a two-story building with four ground-floor garages for motor vehicle repairs and a second floor with barracks space for enlisted soldier mechanics.

Another eleven historic district RTHL candidate properties are privately owned:

POST HEADQUARTERS BUILDING, 1857: Originally built to serve as the commanding officer's quarters, this building became the post headquarters in 1873. Following World War I, in 1919, the building was expanded, doubling its size. In 1939–40, the present exterior was added, surrounding the 1857 and 1919 portions of the building, creating additional office space. Sometime after February 1943, the flat roof was removed and a frame second story was added. On Thanksgiving Day, November 26, 1959, during filming of John Wayne's epic *The Alamo*, the building caught fire—the result of a faulty kerosene heater—and burned. Only the shell remains. The 1857 portion of the building exhibits the finest stone craftsmanship in the district.

QUARTERS NO. 6–7, 1870: A single-story duplex with a *U*-shaped plan, this building was the first officers' quarters built following the reoccupation of the fort after the Civil War and only the second to be made of stone. The report of Acting Assistant Surgeon Donald Jackson, United States Army, July 20, 1870, describes the building in detail. It was used as an officers' mess in the twentieth century.

BLACKSMITH SHOP, 1870s: Post building No. 252. This single-story stone building nestled behind the motor pool is now a well-kept private home. Historically the building saw many uses associated with the Quartermaster Department.

HOSPITAL STEWARDS CABIN, 1874: Post building No. 75. This stone cabin behind the post hospital served as quarters for the hospital steward, perhaps the most important enlisted man on the post after the regimental sergeant major. It then served as a recreation hall for the Women's Army Corps detachment in World War II. The building is now a single-family home.

BACHELOR HALL, 1885: Post building No. 1 was built on a rectangular plan with eight two-room suites for bachelor officers, lettered A–H. It was an impressive two-story stone structure, featuring front and rear porches for each floor and interior stairwells for access to the second floor. The rear porches each had four small rooms, which were converted to bathrooms in the 1920s. The rear porches have since been removed. Rented as the Cavalryman Studio Rooms during the Guest Ranch era (a single was fifteen dollars and a double twenty-eight dollars per night), the building is now eight private condominiums.

QUARTERMASTER WORKSHOPS, 1891: Post building No. 73, completed in November 1891 at a cost of $2,990. Located across from the Guard House, this stone building contained individual rooms for a blacksmith shop, a wheelwright, a paint shop, a plumber and tinner, a saddler and a carpenter shop. Used as a bowling alley in World War II, the building is divided into three spacious homes today.

FRAME OFFICERS' QUARTERS, 1920S: Post building No. 254, Married Officers' Quarters, single set. This is the only surviving example of frame officer quarters in the district.

POST EXCHANGE TAILOR SHOP, 1930S: Post building No. 151. There is not much detail about this building, which operates today as the Rockledge Manor Apartments. Fort Clark's original building No. 151 was the post laundry in 1928. This building also had a restaurant operated by a Chinese Quartermaster Corps employee. Soldiers like to look sharp, so many had their baggy army uniforms tailored to fit at this building.

GARAGES, 1930S: Post building No. T-301 (the *T* signifies "temporary"). This building behind Bachelor Hall is a series of connected three-bay garage sheds constructed of stonemasonry. There are fifteen bays in all, divided by wood frame walls. It seems seven Bachelor Hall apartments each were allocated two garages, while the eighth only got one.

TRIPLEX OFFICERS' QUARTERS, 1942: Post buildings No. T-256, T-257 and T-258. Why it was placed in the "T" category remains a mystery, as it is far from temporary. This building, divided into three housing units, is the last permanent officers' quarters built by the army on the post. Each set

Primary privately owned RTHL candidates: BOQ (*top, left*); Triplex (*top, right*); Civilian War Housing (*center*); Post Headquarters (*bottom, left*); and Quartermaster Workshops (*bottom, right*). *Author's collection.*

had a porch, a living room, a dining room, a kitchen, two bedrooms, a bathroom, a fireplace with electric blowers and a telephone nook—very up-to-date for the 1940s. The Guest Ranch renamed the building the Ranger Apartments, which became popular rental units at sixty dollars per day for four persons.

CIVILIAN WAR HOUSING, 1942: These buildings are an outlier from the historic district but, nonetheless, U.S. Army construction: twenty-five cinderblock two- to three-bedroom duplexes built by the army as housing for civilian workers and noncommissioned officer families during World War II. These quarters were later rental units and referred to as the 49ers during the Guest Ranch era. Only one or two units remain unaltered.

The Fort Clark Municipal Utility District, a Texas special-purpose local government, owns three former U.S. Army structures:

WATER TREATMENT PLANT, 1919: Post building No. 92. A pump house has occupied this site since the 1890s, when water from the spring was pumped to a square wooden tower behind Officers' Row. Still in operation for its intended purpose.

WATER TOWER, 1920: Post building No. 200. Replaced an earlier steel water tower erected in 1902. Still in use.

CONCRETE VEHICLE BRIDGE, 1935–37: Post building No. 201. Between 1935 and 1937, the Works Progress Administration (WPA) replaced the iron wagon bridge that had spanned Las Moras Creek since 1892 with a two-lane concrete vehicle bridge. The foundation of the stone pier from the wagon bridge is still visible in the creek. A bronze WPA plaque is affixed to the north end of the bridge. This bridge is now nearly ninety years old.

A final category of sites is foundation remains of once-significant post facilities and the ghosts of World War II frame construction only identified from photographs and army building numbers on maps. The intrepid visitor will need to explore the brush outside the historic district to find these remnants of U.S. Army construction, many of which have the potential for adaptive reuse.

U.S. ARMY KNOWN DISTANCE (KD) RIFLE RANGE CONCRETE TARGET PIT: Located on the Fort Clark Gun Club sixty-four-acre lease and possibly the only such feature left in Texas.

POST BASEBALL DIAMOND: Post building No. T-157. The grandstand foundation and concrete dugouts remain. Did Jackie Robinson play here when he was briefly stationed at Fort Clark in 1943?

POST THEATER NO. 2: Post building No. T-1338. Of this one-thousand-man auditorium built for the soldiers of the 2nd Cavalry Division, only a large, sloping concrete slab with entrance steps and low walls remains. At little expense, this site could be transformed into an open-air stargazing or assembly venue.

FIRE STATION NO. 2: Post building No. T-1340. The outline of this building remains visible in the old 2nd Cavalry Division cantonment area. A photo of this building appears on page 102 of Arcadia Publishing's *Fort Clark and Brackettville, Land of Heroes* (Images of America series).

POST LAUNDRY: Post buildings No. T-592 and 593. A soaring brick smokestack still overlooks a massive concrete slab where the World War II post laundry facility once stood. The site has been a platted subdivision (Unit 4) since 1973, with dozens of privately owned undeveloped individual building lots set aside for residential use.

VETERINARY HOSPITAL: Post building No. T-596. A large slab with a brick chimney adjacent to the original post cemetery, this site could be made into a trailhead facility for interpretation of the nature trail network and the remains of the 2nd Cavalry Division cantonment area.

POST STOCKADE TOWER: Post building No. T-394. A round three-story concrete tower with cells for confinement of more dangerous prisoners. There is inaccurate, misleading local signage at the site.

ENLISTED BATH HOUSE: Post building No. 296. Concrete foundation on the south bank of Las Moras creek downstream from the swimming pool. Site of a group photo of officers of the 3rd Cavalry and Nineteenth 19th Infantry in 1888. Also the site of the long-standing nineteenth- and twentieth-century footbridge across Las Moras creek, this site has the potential for interpretive signage and/or a picnic table to encourage visitation.

MOTOR POOL FOUNDATIONS: Post buildings No. T-1213, 1221, 1223 and 1225. Long rectangular concrete slabs from maintenance buildings. This is another potential site for interpretive signage and/or picnic tables.

POST DAIRY BARN: Post building No. T-564. Deep in the brush are the remains of a long concrete foundation with a trough down the center. The post dairy farm was a long-established twentieth-century post exchange concession operated by a civilian contractor.

CLASS 60 TIMBER TRESTLE BRIDGE: Post building No. T-1236. There were two of these sturdy bridges across Las Moras creek, which could carry a fifteen-ton M3 Stuart tank. The remaining upper bridge, with decking only down the center, is still in use, now as a footbridge.

POST QUARTERMASTER OFFICES: Post building No. 331. Little remains of this building other than the center foundation walls and a concrete bridge across the drainage ditch in front of the building.

LAS MORAS HEIGHTS WAR HOUSING PROJECT, 1944: Las Moras Heights was a 160-unit housing project of wood frame apartments that opened its doors to civilian war workers and military personnel of the post on March 1, 1944. In addition to the 160 housing units, there were two dormitories,

Gone but not forgotten: post baseball diamond grandstand (*top, left*); dairy barn (*top, right*); 2nd Cavalry Division Auditorium (*center*); offices of the Post Quartermaster (*bottom, left*); and World War II barracks (*bottom, right*). *Author's collection.*

one for women and one for men, and several recreation buildings for the residents. Today the site is occupied by the Bivouac RV Park and an RV storage facility. Three figure-eight concrete roads are all that remain of the 1944 construction.

AMMUNITION BUNKERS: There are six Quonset hut bunkers covered with earth, each having a reinforced concrete front elevation with a heavy iron blast door; they are currently used for storage.

MOBILIZATION 63 MAN BARRACKS, SERIES 700: Dozens of these wood frame buildings familiar to generations of soldiers were constructed at Fort Clark during the mobilization for World War II at a cost of $10,728 each. None remain, as all were torn down during the postwar salvage operation.

I often imagine how a former Fort Clark soldier would react to seeing the fort today. Of course, it would greatly depend on that soldier's era of service. The first constant would be Las Moras Spring, the one familiar place common to every soldier's memory. The walled-in spring pond and huge post swimming pool would certainly be a marvel to the great majority. I think next in order of remembrance would be the trees, those centuries-old forest monarchs along the creek Chaplain Bateman spoke of over a century ago. When a handful of old Buffalo Soldiers from the 2nd Cavalry Division returned to Fort Clark in 2008, each trooper recognized the trees and even used them to orient themselves when visiting their now-invisible overgrown cantonment. As for the buildings, there is no doubt the Guard House would have universal recognition, followed by the building where a given soldier lived and the mess hall where he took his meals. In the 1990s, there was always an annual "Trooper's Reunion" for soldiers of the 5th Cavalry and the 112th Cavalry. One particular 5th Cavalry trooper customarily requested a motel room in Bullis Hall, which had been his barracks in the 1930s. In between activities, he could be found just sitting silently on the porch, surrounded by his memories. Just how would any old Fort Clark soldier judge this place? What kind of shape is it in? Has it been properly cared for? Would it pass inspection? In my mind's eye, I see a soldier in blue or khaki or olive drab standing and reading one of our historical markers, nodding his head, turning toward me and saying, "Well, somebody got that right."

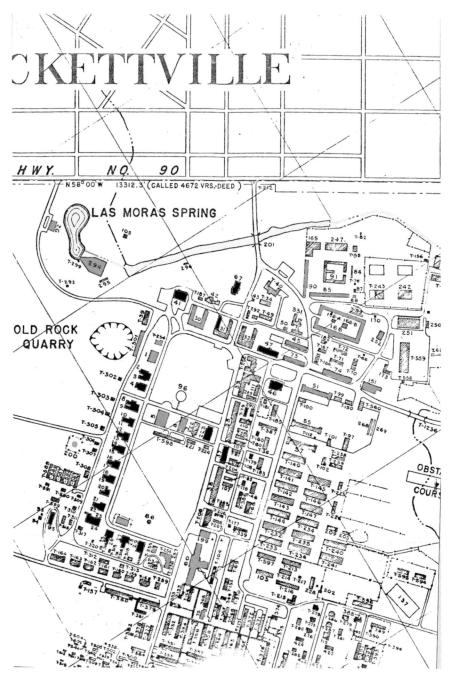

Map of Fort Clark, 1944. Black buildings are RTHLs. Gray buildings are eligible. *Corps of Engineers.*

EPILOGUE

In September 2012, I initiated the three- to five-year nomination process with the Department of the Interior, National Park Service, for designation of the Fort Clark National Register Historic District as a National Historic Landmark, hoping to upgrade the district's status from a Ford to a Rolls Royce. Most National Historic Landmarks are owned by private individuals or groups. Owners are given an opportunity to comment on nominations, and private owners of potential National Historic Landmarks are given the opportunity to concur in or object to their designation. NHL status offers advantages to owners who wish to preserve their properties. It aids decision-making by private organizations and individuals because it is the primary federal means of assessing the national significance of historic properties. A formal survey of the seventy-four property owners in the Fort Clark Historic District resulted in a 96 percent concurrence with the NHL nomination.

A representative of the National Park Service, Intermountain Region, headquartered in Denver, Colorado, visited Fort Clark in March 2014; she was in awe and speechless as she marveled at the extent and condition of the district. She experienced the usual astonishment felt by professional historians when they ask themselves, "How could I not know about this place?" The integrity of the site was convincingly established, putting the district one step closer to designation as a National Historic Landmark. Only six Texas forts currently are designated National Historic Landmarks: Belknap, Brown, Concho, Davis, Richardson and Sam Houston. All are owned and maintained by government entities. Fort Clark survives essentially intact due to the care and commitment of private citizens.

Post Flagpole and garrison flag in 2008. *Photo by author.*

However, I naively underestimated the determination and influence of the only owner of a non-historic property in the district who did not support the NHL nomination. He relentlessly spread vicious, baseless, false rumors among property owners outside the district, convincing them that NHL status would result in the seizure of their property by the federal government, a totally cruel and malicious lie. My wife and I began to receive threats and were confronted in public. Our home was targeted. The situation became so untenable that I was forced to abandon the project with just one step remaining. Tragically, the opportunity was lost.

In the end, nothing can replace the experience of being in the actual historic settings where our national history was shaped. No replica can achieve the genuine connection that historic places give us with our collective past. In Kinney County, Texas, there is an authentic place where Americans can experience their history firsthand. Fort Clark is that place. History still matters, for when we look into the past, we can find ourselves doing remarkable things in the present.

A youngster once asked me, "Hey, old-timer, you know a lot about this place—have you lived here all your life?" I smiled and said, "Not yet!"

BIBLIOGRAPHY

Alexander, Thomas E., and Dan K. Utley. *Faded Glory: A Century of Forgotten Texas Military Sites, Then and Now.* College Station: Texas A&M University Press, 2012.

Almond, Killis P., Jr. *Fort Clark Historic District Preservation Plan.* San Antonio: De Lara-Almond, Architects, 1981.

Austerman, Wayne R. *Sharps Rifles and Spanish Mules: The San Antonio–El Paso Mail 1851–1881.* College Station: Texas A&M University Press, 2000.

Barnard, Edward S., ed. *Story of the Great American West.* New York: Readers Digest, 1977.

Bateman, Cephas C. "History of Fort Clark." *U.S. Army Recruiting News,* November 1923.

———. "Landmark of the Old Frontier Fort Clark, Texas." *Army and Navy Register* 54, no. 1744 (December 1913).

———. *Modernized Outpost of the Old Frontier.* Fort Clark: 13th Cavalry Printing Office, 1920.

Billings, John S. *Circular No. 4: A Report on Barracks and Hospitals, with Descriptions of Military Posts.* War Department, Surgeon-General's Office. Washington, D.C: Government Printing Office, 1870.

———. *Circular No. 8: A Report on Hygiene of the United States Army with Descriptions of Military Posts.* War Department, Surgeon-General's Office. Washington, D.C.: Government Printing Office, 1875.

Bliss, Zenus R. *The Reminiscences of Major General Zenas R. Bliss, 1854–1876: From the Texas Frontier to the Civil War and Back Again.* Edited by Thomas Ty

Smith, Jerry Thompson, Robert Wooster and Ben E. Pingenot. Austin: Texas State Historical Association, 2008.

Blumenson, Martin. *The Patton Papers: 1885–1940.* Boston: Houghton-Mifflin, 1972.

Boyd, Frances Anne Mullen. *Cavalry Life in Tent and Field.* New York: J. Selwin Tait & Sons, 1894.

Boylan, Abigail Robenson. "My Love Affair With Fort Clark." Edited by William F Haenn and Chris A Hale. *Fort Clark Post Return* (Friends of the Fort Clark Histroic District) 3, no. 1 (Summer 2009): 1–2.

Brown, William L., III. *The Army Called It Home: Military Interiors of the 19th Century.* Gettysburg, PA: Thomas Publications, 1992.

Burleson, Clyde W., and E. Jessica Hickman. *The Panoramic Photography of Eugene O. Goldbeck.* Austin: University of Texas Press, 1986.

Carlson, Paul H. *"Pecos Bill": A Military Biography of William R. Shafter.* College Station: Texas A&M University Press, 1989.

Carson, James. *Against the Grain: Colonel Henry M. Lazelle and the U.S. Army.* Denton: University of North Texas Press, 2015.

Conger, Roger N. *Frontier Forts of Texas.* Waco: Texian Press, 1966.

Conway, Walter C. "Colonel Edmund Schriver's Inspector-General's Report on Military Posts in Texas, November, 1872–January 1873." *Southwestern Historical Quarterly* (Texas State Historical Association) 67, no. 4 (April 1964).

Crimmins, Colonel Martin Lalor. "Colonel J. K. F. Mansfield's Report of the Inspection of the Department of Texas in 1856." *Southwestern Historical Quarterly* (Texas State Historical Association) 67, no. 2 (1938): 122–48.

———. "W. G. Freeman's Report on the Eigth Military Department." *Southwestern Historical Quarterly* (Texas State Historical Association) 53, no. 1 (1949): 71–74.

Deed Records. Vols. A–5. Kinney County, Texas: Mary Maverick to the United States of America, December 11, 1883.

Deed Records. Vols. A–34. Kinney County, Texas: United States of America to the Texas Railway Equipment Company, October 29, 1946.

Deed Records. Vols. A–42. Kinney County, Texas: Texas Railway Equipment Company to the Brown Foundation, May 10, 1967.

Deed Records. Vols. A–43. Kinney County, Texas: The Brown Foundation to North American Towns of Texas, Inc., May 21, 1971.

"Description of Post of Fort Clark, Texas." QMD Form 3-21, 1901.

Eales, Anne Bruner. *Army Wives on the American Frontier, Living by the Bugles.* Boulder, CO: Big Earth Publishing, 1996.

Ferris, Robert G. *Soldier and Brave: Historic Places Associated with Indian Affairs and the Indian Wars in Trans-Mississippi West.* Washington, D.C.: US Department of the Interior, 1971.

"Fort Clark Texas." *Souvenir Picture Booklet.* Fort Clark, TX: Fort Clark Public Relations Office, 1943.

Fort Clark, Texas. Map, Record Group 77, Miscellaneous Forts File, Washington, D.C.: National Archives and Records Administration, 1920.

French, Francis Henry. "The Diary and Letters of Lieutenant Francis H. French, 19th Infantry, at Fort Clark Texas, 1883–1888." Compiled by William F Haenn. Vinton Trust, unpublished manuscript.

Grashof, Bethanie C. *1866–1890*, Vol. 2 of *A Study of United States Army Family Housing Standardized Plans, 1866–1940.* Center for Architectural Conservation, College of Architecture, Atlanta: Georgia Institute of Technology, 1986.

Haenn, William F. *Fort Clark and Brackettville, Land of Heroes.* Images of America series. Charleston, SC: Arcadia Publishing, 2002.

———. "Gallant Company 'Q,' The Post Guard House on the Western Frontier." *On Point: The Journal of Army History* (Army Historical Foundation) 28, no. 1 (Fall 2022): 18–25.

Haines, Major O.L., ed. "Border Cavalry Stations—Fort Clark, Texas." *Cavalry Journal* (United States Cavalry Association) 39, no. 161 (October 1930): 512–16.

Hart, Herbert M. *Old Forts of the Southwest.* Seattle: Superior Publishing, 1964.

Haynes, David. *Catching Shadows: A Directory of 19th-Century Texas Photographers.* Austin: Texas State Historical Association, 1993.

Heitman, Francis B. *Historical Register and Dictionary of the United States Army, From Its Organization, September 29, 1789, to March 2, 1903.* Washington, D.C.: Government Printing Office, 1903.

Hoagland, Alison K. *Army Architecture in the West, Forts Larmie, Bridger, and D.A. Russell, 1849–1912.* Norman: University of Oklahoma Press, 2004.

Johnson, Hugh S. *The Blue Eagle from Egg to Earth.* New York: Doubleday, 1935.

Kendall, Major Henry F. *Description of Post of Fort Clark.* Form 3-24, U.S. Quartermaster Department, 1901.

Kimball, Maria Brace. *A Soldier-Doctor of Our Army—James P. Kimball, Civil War, Indian Wars, Spanish War.* Boston: Houghton Mifflin, 1917.

Lane, Lydia Spencer. *I Married a Soldier, or Old Days in the Old Army.* Philadelphia: J.B. Lippincott, 1893.

Lauderdale, John Vance. *An Army Doctor on the Western Frontier: Journals and Letters of John Vance Lauderdale, 1864–1890.* Edited by Robert M. Utley. Albuquerque: University of New Mexico Press, 2014.

Laurence, Mary Leefe. *Daughter of the Regiment, Memiors of a Childhood in the Frontier Army, 1878–1898.* Edited by Thomas T Smith. Lincoln: University of Nebraska Press, 1996.

Mansfield, Joseph K.F., and Joseph E. Johnston. *Texas & New Mexico on the Eve of the Civil War.* Edited by Jerry D Thompson. Santa Fe: University of New Mexico Press, 2001.

Maverick, Mary A., and George M. Maverick. *Memoirs of Mary A. Maverick: A Journal of Early Texas.* Edited by Rena Maverick Green and Maverick Fairchild Fisher. San Antonio: Maverick Publishing, 2005.

McKinnon, Maynard Hill. "The Letters from Fort Clark, Texas Written by Maynard Hill McKinnon to His Fiancé Josephine Ann Stears, July 1917 to March 1918 during his U.S. Army Service in Ambulance Company No. 7." Edited by William F Haenn. Unpublished manuscript.

Miller, Ray. *Texas Forts: A History and Guide.* Austin, TX: Cordovan Press, 1985.

Moffitt, Lester W. "Historic Fort Clark Remodeled—Landmarks of Indian Warfare Dot Reconstructed Military Reservation." *United States Army Recruiting News,* July 1938.

National Register Narrative—Fort Clark Historic District. National Register of Historic Places Listing, National Park Service, Washington, D.C.: U.S. Depatment of the Interior, 1979.

Office of Constructing Quartermaster. "Plan of Fort Clark Texas Showing Existing Structures and Utilities." Surveyed, compiled and drawn by Wm. B. Fuller. Map, Fort Clark, Texas, 1918.

O'Harrow, Robert Jr. *The Quartermaster: Montgomery C. Meigs, Lincoln's General, Master Builder of the Union Army.* New York: Simon & Schuster, 2016.

"Outline Descriptions of the Posts in the Military Division of the Missouri Commanded by Lieutenant General P. H. Sheridan." Map, Chicago, 1876, 184–86.

Overman, Captain L. Cooper. "Plan of Fort Clark." Map. San Antonio: Office of the Quartermaster, Department of Texas, 1871.

Paulding, William. "My Life in the Army, 1873 to 1907." Edited by David Paulding Gose. Unpublished manuscript, 1994.

Pingenot, Ben E. "Fort Clark, Texas, A Brief History." *Journal of Big Bend Studies* 7 (January 1995): 103–22.

Plan and Specifications of Commanding Officers Quarters. Fort Clark, Texas, Record Group 77, Miscellaneous Forts File, Washington, D.C.: National Archives and Records Administration, 1873.

Plan and Specifications of Company Officers Quarters. Fort Clark, Texas, Record Group 77, Miscellaneous Forts File, Washington, D.C.: National Archives and Records Administration, 1873.

Plan and Specifications of Guardhouse. Fort Clark, Texas, Record Group 77, Miscellaneous Forts File, Washington, D.C.: National Archives and Records Administration, 1873.

Plan and Specifications of Soldiers Barracks. Fort Clark, Texas, Record Group 77, Miscellaneous Forts File, Washington, D.C.: National Archives and Records Administration, 1872.

Plan of Fort Clark Shops. Fort Clark, Texas, Record Group 77, Miscellaneous Forts File, Washington, D.C.: National Archives and Records Administration, 1891.

Plan of Hospital. Fort Clark, Texas, Record Group 77, Miscellaneous Forts File, Washington, D.C.: National Archives and Records Administration, 1873.

Plan of Hospital Steward's Quarters. Fort Clark, Texas, Record Group 77, Miscellaneous Forts File, Washington, D.C.: National Archives and Records Administration, 1873.

Plan of Quartermasters Store-House. Fort Clark, Texas, Record Group 77, Miscellaneous Forts File, Washington, D.C.: National Archives and Records Administration, 1892.

Pogue, Forrest C. *George C. Marshall: Education of a General 1880–1939.* New York: Viking Press, 1963.

"Post Return, Fort Clark, Texas." Microcopy M617, Roll 215, Manuscript Division, National Archives and Records Administration, Washington, D.C., December 1886.

Pourie, Colonel James R. *Report of Inspection of Buildings and Utilities at Fort Clark, Texas.* San Antonio: Headquarters 8th Corps Area, 1928.

Pratt, Joseph A., and Christopher J. Castaneda. *Builders: Herman and George R. Brown.* College Station: Texas A&M University Press, 1999.

Railsbach, Thomas C. *The Drums Would Roll: A Pictorial History of U.S. Army Bands on the American Frontier, 1866–1900.* London: Arms and Armour Press, 1987.

Register of Graduates and Former Cadets of the United States Military Academy. West Point: West Point Alumni Foundation, 1965.

"Returns of Military Posts—Fort Clark, Texas." Microcopy M617, Roll 213, Manuscript Division, National Archives and Records Administration, Washington, D.C., 1852–1916.

Salvant, Joan U., and Robert M. Utley. *If These Walls Could Speak—Historic Forts of Texas.* Austin: University of Texas Press, 1985.

Smith, Thomas T. *The Old Army in Texas: A Research Guide to the U.S. Army in Nineteenth-Century Texas.* Austin: Texas State Historical Association, 2020.

————. *The U.S. Army & the Texas Frontier Economy, 1845–1900.* College Station: Texas A&M University Press, 1999.

Stallard, Patricia Y. *Glittering Misery: Dependents of the Indian Fighting Army.* Norman: University of Oklahoma Press, 1992.

Steely, James Wright. *A Catalog of Texas Properties in the National Register of Historic Places.* Austin: Texas Historical Commission, 1984.

Sullivan, Captain Charles J. *Army Posts & Towns: The Baedeker of the Army.* Burlington, VT: Free Press Interstate Printing, 1926.

Swanson, Donald A. *Chronicles of Fort Clark.* Austin: Nortex Press, 2003.

Swift, Roy L., and Leavitt Corning Jr. *Three Roads to Chihuahua: The Great Wagon Roads That Opened the Southwest, 1823–1883.* Fort Worth: Eakin Press, 1988.

Taft, William Howard, and Frederick Harris. *Service with Fighing Men: An Account of the Work of the American Young Men's Christian Associations in the World War.* Two vols. New York: Association Press, 1922.

Totten, James Patton, and Ruth Ellen Patton Totten. *The Button Box: A Daughter's Loving Memoir of Mrs. George S. Patton.* Columbia: University of Missouri Press, 2005.

U.S. Army Corps of Engineers. *Context Study of the U.S. Quartermaster General Standardized Plans 1866–1942.* Aberdeen Proving Ground, MD: U.S. Army Environmental Center, 1997.

United States Engineer Office. "Fort Clark Texas General Plan." Map, San Antonio District, Fort Sam Houston Texas, 1944.

Wiggins, Robert Peyton. *Jungle Combat with the 112th Cavalry: Three Texans in the Pacific in World War II.* Jefferson, NC: McFarland, 2011.

Williams, R.H. *With the Border Ruffians: Memories of the Far West, 1852–1868.* Lincoln: University of Nebraska Press, 1982.

Wooster, Robert. *Soldiers, Sutlers, and Settlers: Garrison Life on the Texas Frontier.* College Station: Texas A&M University Press, 1987.

INDEX

ABOUT THE AUTHOR

William Haenn retired from the U.S. Army as a lieutenant colonel in 1993 and has since lived at Fort Clark, immersed in its history. He is the author of the best-selling book *Fort Clark and Brackettville, Land of Heroes*, a photographic history for Arcadia Publishing's Images of America series. His contributions to the military history of the Lower Pecos and Big Bend regions include three feature articles for *On Point: The Journal of Army History*, along with an innovative analysis of two photographs taken at Fort Davis, Texas, in 1887, published in the *Journal of Big Bend Studies*. The Texas Historical Commission honored Bill in 2011 with its prestigious Award of Merit in recognition of his prodigious historical documentation, continued leadership, preservation and heritage tourism promotion of the natural and built environment of Historic Fort Clark, Brackettville, Texas.